A WORTHY CHALLENGE

No group of warriors played a more vital role in any victory than did the U. S. Navy fighter pilots in the key Battle of Leyte Gulf, striving to protect the ships in the gulf as the Jap air force attacked in conjunction with the Jap fleet . . .

In the thick of the fighting was Commander David McCampbell and his "Fabled Fifteen," patrolling the Philippine Sea.

"Look at the flock of bandits, ten o'clock low," suddenly crackled McCampbell's radio. "Sixty Jap planes in the formation—twenty bombers and forty fighters!"

"Only damned fools would jump a bunch like that with the odds better than eight to one," another voice cut in.

"You're right," McCampbell agreed. "Okay, guys, let's go and get 'em!"

AUTHOR'S PROFILE

Jack Pearl was born in New York City and received his B.A. and M.A. degrees at Columbia. He served for thirty months overseas with the Military Police of the U. S Army in Africa, Sicily and Italy.

He started out to be an engineer but soon decided that writing held more promise for him. During his varied literary career, he has been a writer on the Gangbuster TV show, an advertising copywriter and was formerly managing editor of Saga and Climax magazines.

He is the author of innumerable magazine stories and articles as well as the two Monarch Americana bestsellers GENERAL DOUGLAS MacARTHUR and BLOOD-AND-GUTS PATTON.

THE MONARCH AMERICANA SERIES

A Monarch Americana Book

AERIAL DOGFIGHTS OF WORLD WAR II

Jack Pearl

Author of GENERAL DOUGLAS MacARTHUR

MONARCH BOOKS, INC.

Derby, Connecticut

AERIAL DOGFIGHTS OF WORLD WAR II

A Monarch Americana Book

Published in May, 1962

Copyright © 1962 by Jack Pearl

Photographs from Wide World Photos

Monarch Books are published by MONARCH BOOKS, INC., Capital Building, Derby, Connecticut, and represent the works of outstanding novelists and writers of non-fiction especially chosen for their literary merit and reading entertainment.

Printed in the United States of America

CONTENTS

PART ONE

The Day England Was Saved

1.

FLIGHT LIEUTENANT WALTER HEWES bent over the austere wooden washstand and slopped warm water over his face with cupped hands. As he toweled his face briskly, he heard the door of his room slam. He peered out of the folds of damp terry cloth at his roommate, Pilot Officer Bobbie Wadsworth.

Hewes grunted a hello and slung his towel over a hook on the wall. "You going into the village before or after supper, old man?"

Bobbie Wadsworth sat down heavily on one of the twin beds in the small immaculate room. "Neither. The whole squadron's restricted to base tonight. Tomorrow, too."

Hewes whirled and hurled the comb down on the floor in childish tantrum. "What the bloody hell are they trying to do! I've been setting this pigeon up for six weeks. Spent my whole flight pay on her this month. She'll be waiting for me in a room at the Calderone tonight. I've got it all set up. An intimate little supper, champagne . . ." His voice trailed off in impotent frustration.

She'll be waiting a long time," Wadsworth said drily.

"The hell with them!" Hewes exclaimed. "I'll go with or without the Old Man's permission. Damned old tyrant. I just came off a twelve-hour tour of duty."

"Don't bite my head off, buster. Tell it to Colonel

Welch. He wants to talk to the squadron in the mess in fifteen minutes."

Still swearing in uninterrupted outrage, Flight Lieutenant Hewes struggled into the tailored blue blouse of the Royal Air Force. "I'll listen to what he has to say, but it won't make any difference. I'm going to town tonight, and have my little cuddle whether Welch likes it or not."

"Don't blame the Old Man. He takes his orders from the top like everybody else."

"I don't care if he gets them straight from the King himself."

Hewes laughed and threw a friendly arm about his roommate's shoulders. "Don't be a bad sport, laddie."

"Bad sport!" Hewes said bitterly. "This squadron's been swatting Jerries out of the sky like flies. I haven't been off base in six days. There's just so much you can stretch a spring or a man—then *twang*, they've had it."

The date was September 13, 1940. The time was 1830 hours—six-thirty P.M.

The mess hall of the 601st (County of London) Fighter Squadron was a long room crowded with regular rows of rough-plank tables and benches. There was a cold, geometric bleakness about it when it was empty. But at mealtimes, when the blue-jacketed, ruddy-faced youngsters sat shoulder to shoulder at the tables and the high ceiling echoed their exuberant voices and laughter, the room took on the warm, convivial atmosphere of a college fraternity house. If it had not been for the war, a majority of these fighting men would have been sitting at college fraternity tables that night.

"*Atten-shun!*" someone bellowed as Squadron Leader Welch entered from a side door. The talking and laughter ceased as abruptly as if someone had dismissed a radio program with a flick of a knob. There was a scuffle of shoe leather and the protesting rasp of bench legs against splintered floor boards as the squadron rose en masse.

"At ease!" said Colonel Welch in a self-conscious voice. It was difficult for a man of twenty-four years of age to accommodate himself to such demonstrations of obedient respect; it was even more embarrassing to hear himself referred to as the "Old Man."

"Sit down, gentlemen," he told them rather irritably. Informally, the CO hoisted himself onto the serving counter at the front of the mess hall.

When everyone was settled down, he began to speak: "Last July Adolf Hitler gave a victory speech at the Sports Palace in Berlin. In this speech he promised the German people that September fifteenth, he would broadcast to them from Buckingham Palace." He frowned as a nervous titter made the rounds of the RAF boys. Then he said more sharply, "This is no laughing matter. Intelligence has informed us that there is every reason to believe that Hitler intends to keep that promise—give or take a few days.

"Big things are going on across the Channel. Both from recon photos and from intelligence reports, we know that the Germans are massing the greatest invasion armada in history at Calais, Ostend, Dunkirk, Cherbourg, Lorient, Antwerp, Le Havre; even little fishing villages have been commandeered for smaller craft. At this moment there are fifty big merchantmen crammed into Le Havre Harbor alone.

"For a week now, we know that special trains, bristling with armed guards, have been shuttling back and forth between the Fatherland and the French seacoast. We believe that those trains are transporting Hitler's invasion army. Our agents at Dunkirk say that shipfitters are working twenty-four hours a day, converting barges and tugs; when they ram onto a beach, the bow falls away

9

and tanks slip out one after another like kittens out of a cat's belly. Somewhere between fifty and a hundred thousand troops are already aboard transports.

"I don't have to tell you men that in the past two weeks the Nazi air blitz has been stepped up fivefold. Some of you haven't changed your socks for days. Now we've had it easy for twelve hours, and I realize many of you were looking forward to a few hours in town; to see your girls and what not. You certainly deserve that after the showing you've made the past fortnight. But it's going to have to wait. Tonight, tomorrow, the next few days may decide the fate of the British Empire—of the world.

"Hermann Göring has arrived in France to personally direct the blitz, which he predicts will turn the English people into jelly and render them impotent to defend these shores against the invasion armada. In a matter of hours, the Royal Air Force will face its biggest crisis of the war. G-2 says that fat Hermann's first objective is to wipe London off the face of the earth. I expect there's a few of us in the room who will have something to say about that.

"That's all. May God be with you all."

Squadron Leader Welch hopped nimbly off the counter and strode briskly from the room, ignoring the loud *Atten-shun* that some stuffy sergeant major called out. The pilots ignored it, too, staring at their folded hands on the tables and looking, somehow, much older than they had before this speech.

Pilot Officer Wadsworth cast a sidelong glance at his roommate. "You better skip out before supper if you want to keep that date, old boy. She's probably icing the wine and warming up the bed for you right now."

Flight Lieutenant Hewes shook his head and said dully, "I don't expect I'd be very good in bed tonight."

That night all squadrons at the ring of air stations

around London were on "readiness"—prepared to take off at three minutes' notice.

An atmosphere of unnatural, hysterical gaiety prevailed in the duty room of the 601st Squadron. In one corner of the room, a highly competitive game of darts was being waged; a caricature of Adolf Hitler was painted on the cork board. Two beetle-browed men squinted at a chess board through the steam rising out of their tea mugs. Flight Lieutenant Hewes recklessly upped his partner's three-no-trump bid to six spades at the bridge table. Pilot Officer Bobbie Wadsworth, kibitzing over his shoulder, shook his head disparagingly.

"Lucky thing you fly better than you play bridge," he commented.

Five or six men were huddled around a small radio, listening to the news reports.

All the men wore their flight boots, flying overalls and fleece-lined jackets; their helmets and parachutes were in their planes, lined up at the head of the runway like darning needles poised to take off at the first sign of danger.

A burst of static over the loudspeaker froze Hewes as he had the ace of spades halfway to the table; a dart player posed like a statue of Zeus about to hurl one of his thunderbolts; one of the chess players, in the act of reaching for his rook, started and sent pieces spinning across the board like ten pins.

"*All sections stand by!*" intoned the loudspeaker. "*Four hundred Jerries heading for London. First wave of two hundred crossing the coast between Dover and Dungeness at two-thousand-eighteen hours.*"

While the flight leaders were rallying their crews, Squadron Leader Welch came running into the hangar. He was dressed in his flying togs.

Hewes whistled. "The Old Man's got on all his trimmings. It must be really big to get him out of the sack."

Wadsworth zippered up his jacket. "Four hundred Jerries. This is it, old boy."

The pilots jogged at double time in loose formation in the direction of the planes silhouetted sleekly against the rising harvest moon on the horizon. The service crews, alerted by radio, were revving up the engines, their high-pitched animal whine piercing even the eerie air raid sirens that converged on London from all directions.

Hewes and Wadsworth touched gloves briefly before they went to their separate planes. Hewes vaulted up on the wing of his Hurricane fighter and lowered himself into the cramped cockpit. Two ground crewmen on either side of him fussed like mother hens as they eased him into his parachute and clamped his helmet on.

"Good luck, cobber!" shouted a sergeant with a thick down-under drawl.

Hewes held up three fingers and formed a circle with the odd finger and his thumb. Exactly 240 seconds after the alert had come over the squawkbox, the wheels of his Hurricane left terra firma, and he was hurtling to intercept the Nazi air flotilla descending on London.

Hewes looked to the right and to the left. The sight of the other three planes, flying wing to wing in his flight, was reassuring. He was grateful for the moonlight; the small cockpit of a fighter plane can be a lonely place in the infinite black sky. Not that there was much time for idle thought. There are some forty-odd dials, controls and instruments within the cockpit of a Hurricane which demand the constant attention of a fighter pilot.

Hewes checked his oxygen indicator, air-speed indicator, altimeter, petrol gauge, gyrocompass, gyro horizon, noted one of the phosphorescent green lights on his instrument panel was out, and let his eyes slide automatically through the sequence of checks that had been drummed into him like the ABCs.

The radio crackled to life. Hewes recognized Commander Welch's voice: *"Attention all flight leaders . . . Blue section continue on course to London . . . Red Section north-northeast to Kent . . . They're really pasting one of our new airdromes down there . . . White Section . . ."*

The words blurred in Hewes' ears as he saw a great ball of orange fire dilate over the city ahead.

The pilots in his flight conversed excitedly over the radio:

"Jesus Christ, they're through already!"

"East End docks. They must have hit an ammo ship."

"Or a tanker!"

The thousands of antiaircraft guns that ringed London swung into action, their arching fireballs tracing majestic streaks though the sky. The over-all pattern was an enormous fountain of fire, a formidable canopy of shell and flak to keep the Nazi bombers at bay.

But on this night the German fliers swallowed fear and caution; they had their orders from Air Marshal Göring: *We must destroy London at any cost.*

As the Hurricanes crossed the city limits and climbed above the umbrella of flak, Hewes saw a flight of Heinkel bombers nose down in a suicidal dive on a string of waterfront warehouses, straight into the muzzles of a cordon of gun batteries.

One disintegrated in a flash of blue flame. Another took a hit on a wing and spun out of control. The third and fourth got through and leveled out no more than two hundred feet above ground level, laying their eggs neatly along a half-mile strip of docks.

"Scatter, you laddie bucks!" the flight leader commanded.

The RAF, outnumbered as it was, had discovered that its Hurricanes and Spitfires fared better in air combat by

13

abandoning formation flying and permitting each plane to use its advantage of speed and maneuverability over the Nazi Messerschmitt fighters to the full degree.

"Filthy bastards!" Hewes screamed to himself as a line of Heinkels made a deliberate run on Buckingham Palace, dumping their full load of bombs one after the other. To his left, a German fighter screamed down a street, machine-gunning firefighters and rescue workers.

As it pulled up, he latched on to its tail and let go with all eight of his synchronized guns. The Messerschmitt stumbled, shook itself like a wounded hawk peppered with birdshot, then flipped over on its back and crashed into a burning building.

The city of London was lit up in stark relief by the giant torch of the devastated East End. The docks were a sinuous snake of fire curled along the seacoast. There was an unreal horror about the scene, a glimpse into the inferno, a page out of H. G. Wells' *War of the Worlds*, the final Judgment Day.

The air was thick with tracers, both from the ground and from the clashing Nazi and English planes. Heinkels, Dorniers, Messerschmitts, Spitfires and Hurricanes buzzed through the smoke and fire like giant wasps, circling, diving and crisscrossing each other angrily.

Flight Lieutenant Hewes headed for a growing battle going on above Westminster Abbey, where a flight of Spitfires, outnumbered ten to one, were standing off wild rushes of the German fighters who were trying to clear the way for their bombers.

A Dornier crossed his path and he kicked his rudder hard to spray it with tracers. He yelped with glee as a lucky shot exploded the gas tank and the bomber hurtled down like a meteor. His heart thumped as he saw a small fire blazing at the Palace. Mayfair and Oxford Street were rivers of fire from well-placed incendiaries.

Oh, you bastards! he thought and rushed at full speed

into the battle over the Abbey. The Germans were circling the Spits like the Indians in those American Wild West stories. He broke into their formation and pressed hard on the button atop the control stick.

The Germans did not realize an enemy was among them until the tracers began to rake them. Around and around they went in a frantic conga line with one Hurricane at the end of it. Hewes blew the tail off the ship ahead of him and it flipped over and out of control.

His hand flew to the *emergency boost* button. The sudden pressure on it cut out all engine controls except the throttle and the Hurricane spurted through the air as if it had been catapulted by an invisible hand. A burst of tracers sent the next Heinkel spinning; it broke formation and ran.

Hewes touched the *emergency boost*, and he was on the tail of another. Suddenly, the entire formation scattered like ducks frightened by a sharpshooting hunter.

"Hewes, there's a Messerschmitt on your tail!" a voice warned over the loudspeaker. *"Coming in at five o'clock. Jesus, there's three of 'em!"*

Hewes didn't waste time looking. He gave the Hurricane the *emergency boost* and climbed steeply in a half-loop. At the top of the loop, he rolled in an Immelmann that left him flying right side up again in the opposite direction. Then he kicked hard on the rudder and slid off neatly onto the tails of the planes who had been pursuing him moments before; the hunters became the hunted.

He lined up the middle German in his sights and *squeezed the teat*. There was a quick, short burst and then his guns stopped firing. Hewes cursed. At four hundred rounds a second, a fighter pilot had about forty seconds of actual firing time allotted to him on any given mission.

"I've shot my wad!" he muttered to himself. He

banked and climbed away from the fight, setting a course back to the base.

But on the outskirts of the city he ran into another wave of Heinkels approaching. Tears blurred his vision as he looked back at the proud, defiant, fire-ravaged city. They knocked the Jerries down in scores, but still they came on, relentlessly and ruthlessly.

With sudden determination Flight Lieutenant Walter Hewes, twenty-one years old—who a few hours earlier had been cursing King and country because of a broken date with a promiscuous barmaid—turned his plane and headed straight for the oncoming German bombers.

The heavy Heinkels tried to swerve out of his path when his intention became apparent. Escort fighters dove at him desperately, guns blazing. But the single Hurricane navigated the storm of tracers and in one final spurt of glory crashed head on in the midst of a group of clumsy bombers flying wing to wing. The entire flight of four went up in one gigantic flash of exploding bombs and high-test gasoline.

It was typical acts of courage and dedication like this that saved England and the world.

2.

FOR FOUR DAYS and nights Göring's *Luftwaffe* pounded Britain—London, Dover, Weymouth, Porlock, Eastbourne, Esher; the smallest villages did not escape the Nazi's ruthless attention.

Across the Channel, from Narvik to Brest, Hitler's invasion armada was poised, waiting. And back in Berlin Hitler was waiting, too, pacing the marble floors of the *Reichstag*.

"Any word from Göring?" he would ask his aides a hundred times a day.

Every time the phone rang his heart would leap. This *had* to be it! Fat, pompous Hermann reporting with pride that the RAF had been obliterated; that London had been wiped off the face of the earth; that England had been hammered to her knees; that the way was open for the *Wehrmacht*. The Nazi legions would pour onto the beaches unopposed. But the call from Göring never came. For between Hitler's dream and Göring's air force stood the RAF.

Outnumbered thirty to one, the Spitfires and the Hurricanes waged a David-and-Goliath struggle against vast fleets of Messerschmitts, Heinkels, Dorniers and Junkers.

In those critical days the British pilots did not know what sleep was. A fighter pilot stayed in the air until his gas was gone or his plane shot out from under him. Some of the boys actually lost three ships in one day.

Those who were shot down and were lucky enough to bail out without injury, drifted to earth, hailed the first passing vehicle and hitched a ride to the nearest airdrome. There was always a Spit or a Hurricane warmed up and ready to go.

The German air offensive was three-pronged—directed at the British homeland, the British fleet patrolling the English Channel and the convoys carrying vital supplies and war matériel from America.

In the U.S. Civil War it was fashionable for aristocratic men and women to drive out of Washington of a Sunday afternoon in their carriages and park on ridges overlooking a battlefield to watch the Blue and the Gray kill each other. But that was an old-fashioned war. No one could find any sport in the merciless Battle of Britain—nobody but the English, that is!

The white cliffs of Dover offered a first-class balcony seat for the air battles waged over the Channel. Men, women and children, armed with binoculars and telescopes, would throng to favorite vantage spots on good afternoons to cheer "their lads" to victory—and cry when a Spit or Hurricane exploded in the icy water.

One young British radio reporter made broadcasting history when he took a mobile unit up to a high point at Dover and sat cross-legged on the roof of the truck while he described one of the biggest German aerial attacks on a convoy for millions of breathless listeners to the BBC —listeners all over the world. It was like having a box seat at the Army-Navy game, the seventh game of the World Series, the Wimbledon Tennis Finals. Only this was a game where being runner-up meant death!

Charles Gardner's famous commentary is repeated in part:

"There are seven German dive bombers, Junkers 87's. There's one going down on target now! Bomb! No! He missed the ships, it didn't hit a single ship. There are about ten ships in the convoy, but he hasn't hit a single one and— There! You can hear our antiaircraft going at them now. There are about one, two, three, four, five, six—there are ten German machines dive-bombing the convoy.

"Now the British fighters are coming up. Here they come! The Germans are coming in an absolute steep dive and you can see the bombs leave the machines and knife into the water.

"Here's a Spitfire coming down after them. There's a German going down in flames. Somebody's hit a German and he's coming down in a long streak—coming down completely out of control—a long streak of fire and smoke. And now a man's bailed out by parachute . . . And there the ship goes, SMASH! A terrific column of water, and there goes a Junkers 87. Only one man got out by parachute. . . .

"Now, then, oh, there's a terrible mix-up over the Channel! It's impossible to tell which are our machines and which are Germans. . . . You can hear the little rattles of machine-gun fire. *Crump!* That was a bomb nearby, as you may imagine. . . .

"The sky is patterned with bursts of antiaircraft fire, and the sea is covered with smoke where the bombs have burst, but as far as I can see they have not hit a single ship. . . .

"The antiaircraft guns have put up five or six bursts. . . . Oh, they just got a Messerschmitt! Oh, that was beautiful! He's coming down! You hear the crowd roar? He's finished! He's coming down like a rocket! No, the pilot's not getting out of that one!

"There are two more Messerschmitts up there. I think they are all right. No—there's another man finished! He's going straight down and he's not stopping!

"There are three Spitfires chasing three Messerschmitts! Oh, boy! Look at them going! Oh, look how the Messerschmitts—oh, boy! That was really grand! There's a Spitfire behind the first two. He will get them. Oh, yes! Oh, boy! I've never seen anything so good as this. The RAF boys have really got these Germans typed.

"Our machine is catching the Messerschmitt now. He's got the legs of it, you know. Now right in the sights. Go on, George! You've got him! Bomb! Bomb! . . . Machine guns are going like anything. He's being chased out to sea. I can't see any more, but I think the odds would certainly be on that Messerschmitt catching it. . . . Oh, yes, I see it now. Yes, they've got him."

And in summation, Gardner said with bland British understatement: "Well, that was a most unsuccessful attack on our convoy, don't you know!"

A bright sun barely was able to cut through the pall of smoke that hung over the English countryside on the morning of September 16, 1940. Fires smoldered in London and dozens of big and little towns. But for the first time in ninety-six hours the cacophony of ack-ack guns, exploding bombs, air raid sirens and the whine of diving planes was stilled. The sound of church bells echoing across the land filled the people with cheer and hope as they emerged from subway tunnels and other bomb shelters.

Strewn across the length and breadth of England were the charred and smoldering hulks of Messerschmitts, Heinkels, Junkers and Dorniers, stark memorials of the heroic epic which the men of the RAF had written across the skies in the final climactic twenty-four hours of Hitler's greatest air offensive. One hundred-and-eighty-five enemy planes!

Columns of once proud Nazi airmen trudged along country roads on their way to prison camps, herded together by motley uniformed members of the British home guard—and even farmers armed with pitchforks.

Once inside the PW camps these enemy fliers were shocked and unsettled by their own growing numbers as the day wore on. Could "supermen" have suffered such enormous losses? Hadn't the *Führer* told them that the British were a decadent race, without the will or courage to oppose them? For many a young, haughty German this day must have brought a grim moment of truth. On this day Hitler's empire must have experienced the first faint tremors of the earthquake that would finally send it crashing into oblivion.

The finale of the Battle of Britain was still to come, however.

On September 15, while the Nazi blitz was at its height, British Bomber Command Chief Sir Charles Portal conferred with his wing and group commanders in the bombproof operations room of the Air Ministry deep be-neath the streets of London.

"This is it, gentlemen," he told them calmly. "Hitler's zero hour. His invasion fleet is ready to sail. One hundred and fifty thousand crack Nazi troopers supported by tanks and artillery will storm ashore on English soil tomorrow at dawn unless we can stop them—we and the British Navy."

That night there were almost as many British bombers in the air as there were German bombers over England. They followed the long silvery highway across the Channel painted by a full harvest moon. Below them a line of sleek destroyers and fast gunboats cut silently through the dark water.

"Tonight we raid Calais," Flying Officer Donald Wiggins said to his co-pilot, Sergeant Pilot Lester Brown, as he trimmed the controls of their battle bomber at twenty thousand feet and began the long glide toward the French coast.

Brown nodded silently.

Wiggins glanced covertly at his twenty-year-old co-pilot and felt a twinge of sorrow. A boy, that's all he was! A boy who had never known a woman's body, never been drunk, never enjoyed any of a man's prerogatives except the bitter right to kill or be killed for King and country.

"Kind of gets you in the belly, Brown, doesn't it?"

The boy smiled. "Not as bad as phoning a girl for a date the first time, sir."

Flying Officer Wiggins laughed. "That does take guts, Sergeant, I agree. You're really on your own in a situation like that." He glanced out of the cockpit windows, left and right, at the dark shapes of the planes on either side and below and above, and at the ships on the water, and back toward England where the fires and the ack-ack pyrotechnics marked the battles over London. "We are not alone here, Brown—that's for sure."

The youthful sergeant sighed. "First time I went away to boarding school I bawled the whole night into my pillow. Missed my mum; you know how it is. Funny, that was only six years ago." He turned and looked straight into the officer's eyes. "But I'm not scared or lonely tonight, sir. This is a family affair, this war. Got a brother in a Nazi PW camp. Another a machine gunner, waiting for the Jerries on Brighton Beach. Sis is a Wren. Dad's in home guard. And my mum drives an ambulance."

Wiggins looked at him with new respect and understanding. "Sergeant, I can't think of another man I'd rather have sitting in that seat than you."

"Thank you, sir," Brown mumbled.

The radio began to crackle, and abruptly the night in front of them erupted in fire.

"Here we go!" sang out Wiggins.

Then the French coast was beneath them. Searchlights speared one of the bombers and held it as the Nazi gunners zeroed in on it with tracers. Puffs of red and orange, deceptively pretty and innocent-looking, bracketed the bomber. Then suddenly it was gone in a sheet of white-hot light. The explosion sent Wiggins' bomber bucking like a frightened horse.

"Steady, old girl!" Wiggins pointed downward through the window at the toylike boats jamming the harbor, brightly outlined against the water by the phosphorus flares with their eerie greenish light. Wiggins looked for the lock connecting the river basin to the port; this was his target.

"There she is!" Brown shouted.

One by one, the planes of the squadron followed the leader, peeling off in a sliding, half-turn to the left and down into the heavy ack-ack fire.

"Bombs away! shouted the bombardier as the lock entered the cross-hairs of his bombsight. Minus the heavy load of explosive the plane fairly leaped into the air. Wiggins gave her full throttle, trying to climb and turn away from the deadly fingers of ack-ack creeping toward them.

There was no time to sight-see now, and only the cheers of the crew told him that the bombs had indeed been true.

"Bull's-eye!" shouted Brown. "We got it, skipper!"

Before Wiggins could reply there was an explosion dead ahead, and the nose of the bomber seemed to disintegrate in flying glass and twisted metal. Then they were in a steep twisting dive, down, down, down into the eyes of the searchlights.

Brown, blinded by blood, was fully conscious. Beside him sat Wiggins, a headless horseman, with his hands locked on the controls. His first glimpse of the decapitated pilot sent a rush of vomit shooting from the twenty-year-old sergeant's mouth.

Then, in the next few seconds, his boyhood left him forever. Straining against his seat belt, Brown swung about in his seat and lifted his left leg. With the heel of his boot he knocked the dead hands from the controls. He felt the dual controls on his side respond now. And now he fought the battle of his life against that spin. The wounded bomber reacted sluggishly, determined, it seemed, to commit suicide.

"Steady, girl! Steady!" Brown whispered to her in the manner Wiggins had cooed and cajoled the inanimate monster, as if she were a living, hearing thing.

And it worked. The spin stopped, but they were still plummeting steeply toward those lights which seemed almost close enough to reach out and touch. Brown groaned and pulled back on the stick with all his strength. He closed his eyes to blot out those terrible lights, and waited for the crash. But it never came.

He opened his eyes timidly and the lights were gone. They were racing across treetops with blinding speed.

Now he was aware of the voices of the crewmen in his earphones.

"Close scrape, skipper!"

"Good show, skipper!"

Brown swallowed hard and tried to control his voice. "This is Brown. Skipper's dead."

A moment of terrible silence. Then: "Will we make it, Brownie?"

Brown took a deep breath. "We'll make it, men."

He fought for altitude and headed back toward the sea, clear of the fighting. Calais was an awesome sight, a volcano of flame leaping skyward. Brown looked up and down the coast as they approached the Channel, and as far as he could see it was the same in both directions. Fire and destruction. The Judgment Day. Dozens of Nazi ships careened to and fro on the water, funeral pyres for the doomed legions aboard them.

Those that had run for the open sea before the bombers struck destroyed themselves on mines—their own and those dropped by the first wave of bombers. A few escaped the mines, only to be smashed by the guns and torpedoes of the Royal Navy.

Cherbourg was a Wagnerian nightmare of fire, a perfect circle of hell from the air.

Dunkirk, leveled by the Nazi bombers and rebuilt by Hitler's engineers for the invasion of England, was now leveled once again even worse than the first time.

The Nazi invasion dumps and aerodromes at Brest were vaporized.

A curtain of smoke and fire eclipsed the formidable jetty at Lorient from the sight of the evacuated townspeople huddling on a distant hillside watching the show. Seconds later the smoke and fire lifted and they chorused a reverent *"Mon Dieu!"* The entire complex of stone buildings and wharves had vanished as if by magic.

For three nights Sir Charles Portal's bombers hammered the invasion ports relentlessly. Hitler's invasion fleet was reduced to a jackstraw angle of splintered beams and wet, smoldering wood. A low layer of black smoke hung above the Channel giving it "the atmosphere of the River Styx," as Naval Lieutenant Richard Collins, a gunboat commander, expressed it, "the River Styx in which floated little islands of burning wreckage and the thousands of German soldiers drifting face down and face up on their serene way to eternity."

The Harvest moon was blotted out by the smoke of this gigantic pyre.

Then, on the last night, an unexpected gale churned up the Channel, dispelling the smoke and finishing off the job the bombers had begun. The last of Hitler's barges and ships were smashed against stone jetties and on the rocky beaches of France. The Battle of Britain was over. Never again would the psychopathic paperhanger Adolf Hitler pose a serious threat to the British Isles.

The bombings would continue throughout the war with diminishing frenzy, but it was in that critical month of September, when Hitler lost over twelve hundred aircraft in the skies and more than fifty thousand elite troops in the ports of France, that the back of his Third Reich was broken—and all the mad hopes and dreams exploded—by a handful of men and boys in the blue uniform of the Royal Air Force.

In the historic words of Winston Churchill—the immortal tribute to the RAF—"*Never before in history have so many owed so much to so few.*"

PART TWO

The Battle of Africa

3.

THE NUMERICAL SUPERIORITY of the German Air Force and the close support it gave to ground troops had enabled Hitler's *Wehrmacht* to trample France, the Low Countries, Denmark and Norway and slice deep into the heart of Russia. In Africa Nazi General Erwin Rommel, the famed "Desert Fox," was pounding at the gates of Cairo, and the spring of 1942 was a bleak time in history for the Allies.

In Africa, as in Europe, the *Luftwaffe* ruled the skies, and no one rode the crest of victory more proudly than the young eagles of Rommel's Air Force. Many of them were veterans of the campaigns in Yugoslavia, Greece and Crete, easy victories that had made them aces five and six times over.

Outstanding among them was Colonel Hans Marseille, who had achieved acedom at the age of eighteen when he shot down a French fighter plane in the winter of 1939 in a dogfight over the Maginot Line to rack up his fifth "kill." During the next three years he ran that total up to 100-plus.

Marseille was an oddity among Hitler's automated "supermen." He was born one war too late. *Führer* and the Third Reich were not nearly so important inspirations to the "Pilot of Africa" as they were to most young Germans. Colonel Marseille, like the knights of old and the daring young men who fought in the air during World War I, did battle first for glory.

Like his idol, Baron von Richthofen, the immortal "Red Knight" of Kaiser Wilhelm's air service, Marseille liked to dip his wings to a gallant foe. Enemy airmen who fell into the hands of his squadron were treated royally by the colonel, and always partook of a champagne supper with the squadron that would conclude with rounds of toasts featuring fine French brandy and Havana cigars.

Marseille kept an apartment in Bengazi, Libya, to which he retreated at every opportunity. It was as well appointed as any lodging on the Champs Elysées, and boasted a liquor cabinet and larder that would have made a gourmet's mouth water. Excitement was provided by an array of females that included an Italian general's wife, a Nazi field marshal's daughter, an Egyptian princess and an English newspaperwoman who had defected under the spell of the colonel's virility.

During his frequent and lengthy absences, the lovelorn females kept themselves busy polishing "Hansy boy's" collection of miniature loving cups which decorated the back bar. These cups were another manifestation of Marseille's boyish romanticism, an affectation he had copied from the World War I hero, Von Richthofen.

Every time he scored a kill, Marseille would place an order with a native silversmith in Bengazi for one of the loving cups; each one was engraved with the date the kill was made, the type of enemy craft shot down and other vital statistics.

Hans loved those cups dearly, much to the frustration of his lady friends. Often he would be stretched out on the secluded sun deck of the apartment with the princess or the general's wife or the English girl—he in a brief loincloth, she in little more—and there would be the customary nuzzling and fondling which led to fierce, passionate cooperation by the lady.

Then, abruptly, Hans would rise from her unfulfilled person and stride into the parlor where his cups were displayed. And, with far more tenderness and urgency than he had shown to the flesh-and-blood creature, he would stroke one of the cups sensuously with his finger-tips and murmur softly, "You gorgeous thing, *Lieblich, lieblich.*" Then casually to the woman on the sun deck: "My dear, did I ever tell you how I won this cup? Let's see, it was the Christmas of 'forty-one, right after Pearl Harbor . . ."

And on and on he would drone, much to the displeasure of his mistress. It is only fair to state, however, that before the day was over the lady in question invariably got what she was looking for.

Hans Marseille was more than a dandy, let there be no mistake about that. He was as much a "man's man" as he was a "ladies' man," a tremendous favorite with the pilots of his squadron. Sometimes, though, the colonel's outspokenness about the Reich, Adolf Hitler and General Rommel—hallowed ground to the average Nazi-indoctrinated mentality—made his mates cringe with fear for him. But a man with Marseille's qualifications had privileges, even under fascism.

His memorable meeting with the Desert Fox—and the blunt words that passed between them—was the talk of the Afrika Korps (whispered talk) and eventually reached all the way back to Germany via the grapevine.

Rommel, like so many of his prototypes in England and the United States, stubbornly refused to concede that the airplane was anything more than a supporting weapon for his ground forces. As a consequence, his air force, vastly superior to the Allied air force in the Libya-Egypt Theatre, was strung out the length of the desert line, so many planes being allotted to each ground unit. Worse still, from the standpoint of Marseille and other experienced airmen, was the fact that the flights, squadrons, whatever the case might be, were under the supervision of the individual and far-flung ground commanders.

"That idea is antiquated, sir," Marseille told Rommel. "How can there be any coordination with every self-oriented battalion commander pulling the *Luftwaffe* in his own direction like a bunch of children tugging on the strings of a puppet."

The supreme commander flushed. "My commanders all take their orders from me, Colonel. *I* am the coordinator."

"It's not the same thing at all," Marseille persisted. "The *Luftwaffe* is as much an entity as the British Navy. Wouldn't it be silly for General Montgomery to give orders to the British Navy?"

Rommel was speechless with rage.

"What I mean sir," Marseille went on, "is that the air arm must act in concert with the ground forces, to be sure. But as a whole unit, not split up into loose fragments. I recognize the fact that our beloved *Führer*, and you as his agent, dictate the general strategy of the battle. And, in turn, the *Luftwaffe* must attain whatever objectives you assign to it. But we must attain them in the way we best see fit, not at the direction of some major of artillery who doesn't know a Lufberry from an Immelmann."

Rommel's eyes bulged. "You are dismissed, Colonel!"

"General, I—"

"Dismissed!" Rommel's voice was an ominous hiss.

Two weeks later, in May, 1942, General Rommel's Afrika Korps thundered toward Gazala to put the *coup de grâce* to Britain's shaky Eighth Army guarding Cairo. It looked easy.

Fortunately for the Eighth Army—and the civilized world—General Bernard Montgomery had been less unbending to the arguments of his air chief, Sir Arthur Tedder. Tedder swore he would resign rather than assign his meager air force piecemeal to ground commanders.

"What we have we have to use to best advantage. If we allow them to take us on plane for plane, we're doomed. What we've got to do is weld the air arm into a single bolt of lightning and strike like bloody hell wherever and whenever it's needed."

Montgomery agreed, and in the battle that ensued the men of the RAF not only won their independence for all time, but struck a blow in the cause of airmen all over the world.

As Air Marshal Tedder put it: "Any lingering idea that airpower was simply a useful adjunct of the land forces was finally swept away."

If the battle gave the RAF its finest hour since the battle of Britain, the day was not without glory for the enemy either.

4.

The attack is on!

Rommel's tanks move up under an umbrella of artillery, fire while far ahead the Luftwaffe *crosses the British front lines on their way to pound Montgomery's rear.*

Colonel Marseille's squadron of Focke-Wulf 190's, flying at 25,000 feet, shepherds the formation of Stukas several thousand feet below the fighters. The FW-190's are gray and black with crosses on the wings and black swastikas on the rudders. Their bright yellow noses signify that they are manned by the elite of the German Air Force, every man an ace and better. They cruise at 300 mph.

"Achtung!" *the radio sputters.* "Hier kommen sie!"

Coming in fast on the bombers at two o'clock are the British Spits, looking like a flock of sleek hummingbirds in the distance. More fighters than Marseille has seen at one time since the beginning of the African campaign.

"Spits at two o'clock, twelve thousand feet," he alerts his mates. "Follow me down!"

He flips one wing up, noses the 190 down and shoves the throttle forward. The FW screams into a perpendicular dive, and the rest of the squadron play follow the leader. Marseille wants to intercept the English fighters before they can get at the Stukas. But there is a lump in his stomach. Odds have never worried him before, but this time he has to admit the odds are slightly overwhelming. He roughly estimates that there are at least seventy enemy fighters, gaggles of them at various altitudes, coming in at two o'clock and ten o'clock and twelve o'clock high.

There are exactly sixteen FW-190's in his own squadron, and they are tied to the bombers' apron strings. Marseille's ship is doing better than four hundred now, and gradually he lifts the nose and eases into a wide left turn that will bring him in behind the Spits.

He flashes onto the tail of a flight of four enemy planes, arranged like geese in formation. The maneuverable Spitfires break to the left and right in tight turns. Marseille stands on his left wing and stays with the two on that side. A wing hovers in his sights and he lets go with all of his guns. Tracers bracket it, then he touches the rudder expertly and the stream of 50-caliber slugs sprays the fuselage of the Spit like the stream from a hose. It shudders and then amazingly, the wings and the tail separate the way a toy plane which has been improperly glued together might. In a flash it has dropped out of his line of vision.

Marseille concentrates on the remaining Spit, trying desperately to lose him. At this altitude the English fighter has the advantage of intrinsic mobility, but her pilot is not in the same class with the German.

In desperation the Spit noses into a steep dive to pick up speed. Hans grins, a little sadly for her pilot. The heavier FW can fly rings around the Spit at this game. He follows and rather leisurely lines her up in his sights. Two quick bursts and she explodes in flame, continuing the dive into the desert floor.

Quickly he climbs back to the fight. The sky is criss-crossed with fighter planes, German and English, all darting about in such fast confusion that it is difficult to tell friend from foe.

The bombers lumber straight ahead, without deviation, as the battle swirls about them. Two Spits break through the overextended FW's and rake the tail bomber as they speed in from a three o'clock position and zoom over the formation. Bull's-eye! Smoke pouring from her engines, the bomber falters and side slips out of formation.

Marseille cuts in behind the same Spits as they flash past him. The Spits split-S and dive, and he loses them as his radio begins to spark.

"Break Red Leader!" comes the voice of his wingman, Fanier. There are three Spits on his tail, he observes. He tries to shake them with tight turns without success. He pulls back hard on the stick and climbs almost vertically, then loops up and over in an Immelmann turn. But the Spits stick like flypaper. A burst from one stitches his left wing. Marseille side slips and reverses bank and they shoot by him.

He squeezes off a wild burst as a Spit glides across his nose and scores a lucky hit. She spins out of control.

Number three! It's going to be one of those days. Three more little cups. Maybe more!

But the odds are telling now, and Marseille is worried. Ahead he can only count four of the bombers remaining, out of the original two flights of eight. An FW-190 trailing smoke and fire corkscrews to earth. Wherever he looks, his mates are in trouble, fighting defensively *now for the first time in months. The Spits are all over them, coming in at six and two and twelve, high and low.*

Hitler and Rommel! *Marseille spits between his feet. This could never have happened under a unified air command, he realizes. One mile away, maybe two at the most, there were the Messerschmitts and the Focke-Wulfs flying serenely above the infantry and the tanks with nothing to do. Even if they had any way of knowing the mess his squadron was in, Marseille knows they would be powerless to do anything to help without clearance from the ground commander of their sector. And a fat chance that any Esel infantry major or colonel will release any planes assigned to his sector!*

An FW blurs past him flying in the opposite direction with three Spits on its tail. Marseille recognizes his wingman's ship and stands on his wing to follow them.

He presses the mike button and shouts: "Max! Dive! Dive!"

The FW noses down and begins to pull away from the chasing Spits, too preoccupied with their victim to notice Marseille zooming in behind them, closing the gap fast.

Marseille's finger tightens on the firing button as the tail-end Spit looms up bigger and bigger in his sight. Now! Two bursts and the Englishman flips on his back and breaks away trailing fire and smoke. He gasps as the lead Spit's tracers find the cockpit of Max Fanier's 190. Marseille glances at the instrument panel and is stunned to see his speed is close to four hundred. The ground is looming up fast—too fast.

"Max!" *he shouts into the mike.* "Back on the stick! Hard!"

But Max is beyond hearing, and the 190 continues its relentless dive. Marseille watches in horror as it plows into the sand dunes and explodes with a flash of high-test gasoline.

The Spitfires obsessed with their victim almost don't

make it either. They flatten out a scant few feet above the desert. Marseille is on top of them now and closing in with his guns blasting angrily. They have no place to go; no margin of altitude to perform evasive acrobatics. The only way out is up.

One starts to climb, and as it does, it is silhouetted in spread-eagle fashion in Marseille's sights. Dozens of shells cut it in two and it noses down to crash in the sand.

Number four!

He has the other now. The teat goes down. No tracers. No answer from the guns. Marseilles curses, realizing that he is out of ammunition.

You won't get away, you bastard!

He advances full throttle as the Spit noses up and practically climbs on top of the English ship. For an instant, the two planes actually make contact, the 190's prop biting into the Spit's canopy like a band saw. The Spit rebounds and as it does comes too close to the ground. There is a violent explosion beneath the 190 and she bucks high into the air on its recoil.

Marseille fights the controls and coaxes the coughing engine. The heavy ship shudders, hovers between heaven and earth momentarily, then the props dig into the thin dry air and pull her up to safety.

Sadly, Colonel Marseille turns and heads the plane back to base. His ammo is gone; his gas is low. The battle is lost. The concentration tactics of the British have wiped out his entire squadron and the eight bombers they were escorting. And the Spits are off to another sector to repeat their performance.

5.

Air Marshal Tedder's Royal Air Force had a field day at the battle of Gazala, picking off enemy squadrons, spread piecemeal over the front, at their own time, place and pleasure. Then, with the RAF in undisputed control of the skies, Mongomery's Eighth Army sent the badly shaken Afrika Korps staggering back for the first defeat a German land army had suffered in the war.

Badly clobbered by Montgomery again at El Alamein, the invincible *Wehrmacht* began the long retreat that would ultimately end at Berlin.

What of Hans Marseille and the other proud Nazi aces like him? Ironically the knell of doom for Rommel and Hitler, sounded at Gazala, was Marseille's proudest hour. Five kills! Five more silver cups for the collection. Hans placed the order but he was fated never to see them join his collection. On his next mission, Hans Marseille met the fate of all men who push Lady Luck too hard and too long. In one of those sparring matches with the RAF over the desert, he tried to scare off a Spit pilot in a game of aerial "chicken" and they crashed head on.

No one knows what happened to the collection of cups. It is likely they were divided up between the general's wife, the field marshal's daughter, the Egyptian princess and the English newspaperwoman.

It was almost a full year after Pearl Harbor, and the resulting U. S. declaration of war against Germany and Italy as well as Japan, that U. S. forces got in their first licks against the Axis in Europe. More precisely, the U. S. offensive began in Africa with the combined British-American landings at Oran, Algiers and Casablanca.

On November 11, 1942—three days after the invasion had commenced—advance elements of the 33rd Fighter

Group were catapulted from the flight deck of the U. S. carrier *Archer*. It was the first time in aviation history that land-based army planes had ever been deployed from a aircraft carrier.

In charge of the group was a young major by the name of Phil Cochran. Major Cochran, tall, handsome, with close-cropped, prematurely gray hair, looked as if he had been type cast by a Hollywood studio.

His orders were to hop across the Allied airfields in Africa to the Middle East, destination Palestine. Upon their arrival the boys of the 33rd found there was no action in the Middle East at that time, and no prospect of any until the African campaign had been concluded. Disgusted, Cochran and his men piled into their P-40 Warhawks and flew back to Rabat.

Infuriated by his insubordination, the brass of the Twelfth Air Force relieved Cochran of his command and grounded him. But before the order could be made official, Major Cochran hopped into his P-40 and took off for the Tunisian front.

With his fuel running low, he dropped down on a small God-forsaken air strip where a number of Warhawks were scattered about idly. As he jumped down off the wing, a captain gave him an unenthusiastic salute.

"Who's in command here, Captain?" Cochran asked.

The captain scratched his head. "I dunno. I suppose I am."

Cochran's eyes narrowed. "You suppose? What the hell are you guys doing out here anyway?"

"I don't rightly know, Major. They sent us out here; then they must have forgotten about us. We're still waiting for orders."

Cochran exploded. "Good God! Do you guys know there's a war going on up there? And right now it ain't going so good for our side! Those P-40's sitting out there might just as well have been shot down by the Jerries for all the good they're doing the cause."

"Yes, sir." The captain was humble. "By the way, who are you sir?"

Cochran took a deep breath. "I, buddy, am your new commanding officer."

Whipping his "adopted" command into shape was no easy job. The squadron was short on planes, fuel and replacement parts.

"We sure aren't going to last very long if we slug it out with the Jerries and the Eyeties man to man. The way things are, we're going to have to fight like guerrillas," Cochran briefed his squadron. "Hit and run. Get the bastards on the ground. Strafe their convoys, supply dumps, motor pools. But remember, don't get brave with their *Luftwaffe*. He who fights and runs away—well, you know the rest."

In the days and weeks that followed, Major Cochran and his "Red Scarf Guerrillas," as they were tabbed by the harassed Axis, made life miserable for the Germans and Italians who traveled Tunisia's roads through open, exposed desert wasteland. There was no place to hide when Cochran's Warhawks came hedge-hopping across the dunes and ridges the way early American Indians had ambushed wagon trains on the prairie.

"Bonanza!" Cochran would yell into the mike as he led the first pass down the column of trucks and weapons carriers, all piled high with ammunition, shells and other matériel. Down below, the German and Italian drivers scurried away from their vehicles like frightened ants.

The German guards on the vans threw up their rifles or leaped to man the machine guns swivel-mounted behind the cabs. Cochran's 50-calibers opened up and raked the length of the column in seconds. The heavy slugs tossed the Germans about like rag dolls and drilled neat rows of holes that bisected the cab roof of each truck.

Behind Cochran came Captain Levi Chase. One of his 50's caught a bomb just right and the entire load of shells blew skyward, spraying fire up and down the column.

"Good shot, baby!" Cochran congratulated Chase.

The other pilots were furious.

"Hadda hog the whole show for yourself, didn't you, pal?"

Cochran laughed. "Easy, you guys. There's plenty more where that one came from!"

In a chorus: "Let's get 'em then!"

And off they would sail to search out more victims.

Sometimes it would be a huddle of tanks patrolling a desolate district. At the first sight of the P-40's the turrets would clang shut and they would scatter like slow, awkward beetles with a flock of bluejays after them.

The tanks would be lost in the swirls of sand kicked up around them by the 50-calibers. The heavy slugs would batter their armored plate, ineffectively for the most part. But under the saturation of lead, sooner or later a slug would find a weak spot in a tread or welded seam.

Once a stray bullet went through a gun slit and detonated a shell or grenade inside the tank. The steel monster split and ballooned like a blowfish. German crewmen tumbled out of the smoking hatch to die in the burning sand.

"Altogether we must have destroyed about three hundred trucks," Cochran estimates. "We became so damn efficient in this type of work that the Jerries and Eyeties weren't able to move a truck anywhere in Tunisia by daylight."

Once, he relates, they spotted three or four horse-drawn carts loaded with hay.

"We have no fight with the poor Arab farmers," Cochran radioed to his boys. "Let's go."

"Uh-uh, boss," Captain Chase demurred. "I smell Germans."

With that Chase dove on the caravan and pumped a burst into the rear wagon's mound of hay. The wagon blew up like a box of fireworks.

"See what I mean?" Chase radioed back.

Despite their success, the Red Guerrillas did a slow burn when German propaganda broadcasts beamed their way taunted them for being "cowards, who turned tail the moment a Messerschmitt fighter plane put in an appearance."

Major Cochran had to really hold the reins tight after one of these sessions. "Don't you lunkheads realize what they're trying to do is get us so mad we lose our perspective and walk into a fight we have no chance of winning? Stay loose. Our day will come."

And it did before too long, as the American Army and Air Force began to arrive in Tunisia in force.

One day Cochran told his men, "Okay, this is it. Today we're going to go looking for a fight."

They found it pretty quick, too—two flights of Nazi Junkers, escorted by thirty Messerschmitts.

"Bandits at one o'clock low!" Cochran alerted the squadron. "Follow me down!"

The sixteen P-40's peeled off in the steep split-S dives, keeping the sun behind them. They swept down on the enemy bombers from a two o'clock angle raking the formation with deflection shots as they flew straight through it and out the other side.

One of the big mistakes made by the Germans, as well as the Allied fighters, in the early stages of the war was that they stuck too close to their charges, with the result that the bombers were usually under attack before the fighter escort could intervene.

Before the gaggle of Messerschmitts were in action, the Red Guerrillas had sent three of their Junkers flapping earthward like wound ducks.

Two Messerschmitts latch onto Cochran's tail as he flashes past them, but the speed of his dive takes him out of danger. He climbs and turns in a sweeping right turn.

The other P-40's are mixing it up with the 109's now, giving them a two-to-one edge. Chase is on the tail of one German, with two more on his own tail.

He calls for help: "Mayday! Mayday! Can't shake these bandits loose!"

"Break right!" he shouts to Chase, as the two 109's behind his boy open up.

Chase spins the P-40 on the proverbial dime, but the Messerschmitts hang on. Cochran comes in at them now from five o'clock. The swastika on the rudder of the higher one slides into his sight. He gets off a long burst and grins as the "twisted cross" goes to pieces, and the rudderless 109 careens out of control.

It follows its sister ship, the one blasted by Chase, down in a long curl of black smoke. The remaining German tries to run with Cochran on his tail. The powerful 109 loops and rolls, then tries to slide down on Cochran's rear.

"Let him think he's got you!" Chase says over the mike, as he banks and comes around.

Cochran plays possum and the eager German comes on fast at six o'clock. He forgets to check his rear-view mirror. And then it is too late as Chase is all over him, guns spraying the 109 from stem to stern.

He banks sharply as debris from the disintegrating ship whips back in the slipstream rattling against his P-40 like hail.

"That was for Axis Sally!" he sings out merrily to Cochran.

Elsewhere in the sky the other Red Guerrillas are

roughing the Germans up just as badly. At last, with seven planes down, the Messerschmitts break off the fight and chase after their bombers, only specks on the horizon now.

"Let 'em go!" Cochran says.

Gas and ammo are low, and he knows they will run into another reception committee over Allied lines.

Starting with that day, the Red Guerrillas went on a wild rampage that lasted four additional days. In the end, they counted thirty-five kills, Captain Levi Chase accounting for an even dozen of them.

By April 15, 1942, the battle for Africa had been won decisively. Rommel was squeezed from the east and south by Montgomery's Eighth Army and Patton's Second Corps, and the Germans were putting on their own version of the Dunkirk evacuation at Bizerte.

Phil Cochran's Red Guerrillas had figured prominently in the victory with their wholesale destruction of Axis supply columns and dumps behind the lines.

Cochran, himself, was to go on to further fame as the model for "Flip Corkin," the swashbuckling soldier of fortune in Milton Caniff's universally read comic strip *Terry and the Pirates.*

PART THREE

The Battle of the Pacific

6.

The fact that five out of six of the top American air aces in World War II were from the Pacific Theater is no reflection on the prowess of the airmen who fought the *Luftwaffe*. Rather, the average fighter pilot in the Pacific got his baptism of fire earlier in the war than his European counterpart.

General Claire Chennault's "Flying Tigers," for example, were shooting down Jap Zeros and Mitsubishi bombers six months before Pearl Harbor.

Claire Chennault—ex-Army Air Corps captain and barnstorming stunt pilot—was a Louisiana school principal in 1937 when he received an amazing offer from the Chinese Nationalist Government. Still hanging on after five years of devastating war with the Japanese, the Chinese offered Chennault full command of the pathetic Nationalist Air Force with a colonel's commission. Chennault accepted, and in July of that year arrived at Kunming Field to begin what must have seemed like an impossible task.

His command consisted of less than two dozen antiquated fighter planes and bombers and an even smaller number of qualified pilots—mostly foreign mercenaries.

In those dark days China was virtually isolated from the sympathetic democracies of the world by the tentacles of the Japanese Army. There was only one tenuous route through which the United States, England and the passive partners of Chiang Kai-shek could pump supplies into faltering China—the famous Burma Road, a seven-hundred-mile serpentine course that hugged cliffs, climbed mountains and wound through swamp and jungle. Chennault's job was to keep that lifeline open.

Considering what he had to work with, Colonel Chennault did a remarkable job with the Chinese Air Force, but it never gave the Japanese any serious competition. After three years of playing the boy with his finger in the dike, Chennault informed Washington that China was doomed unless it got something more than moral support from the U.S.

Soon after this the United States "sold" Nationalist China one hundred Curtis P-40 Tomahawks. More important, Chennault was given the green light to enlist American "volunteers" from our own armed services to fly the P-40's. The pay was good—$600 a month and a $500 bonus for every Jap plane knocked out of the sky. In July, 1941, the first contingent of the American Volunteer Group (AVG) sailed for Rangoon, first stop on the big trek across "The Hump" to Kunming Field in China.

The group included such celebrities-to-be as Gregory (Pappy) Boyington, first man to crack Eddie Rickenbacker's World War I record of twenty-six kills, and winner of the Congressional Medal of Honor.

There was Bob Smith, first American pilot in World War II to achieve acedom; Jim Howard, another Medal of Honor winner. And there were the boys who would never come home again; John Newkirk, Bob Little, John Petah, Lou Hoffman and Bob Sandell.

At Kunming Chennault hammered his mercenaries into three squadrons, bringing them along slowly and patiently. This patience would pay off later, but it frustrated the AVG in the beginning. They were itching for a fight, but every time the Japs came over, Chennault would send his P-40's scurrying away from the field into hiding.

"The oldest axiom of war is that when an inferior force is up against a superior one, the only chance it has to win is to pick the time and place to fight," Chennault lectured his men. "You'll get your fight, boys, but not until I think you're ready for it."

In addition to being badly outnumbered, the AVG was definitely outclassed in equipment. The Zero fighter, star of the Japanese air service, was a faster, more maneuverable craft than the P-40 Tomahawk, and it commanded a far higher altitude.

"We had an old horse when I was a boy," Chennault told his men a parable. "This horse had the fastest getaway of any animal I ever saw, but he couldn't run a half-mile without getting winded. The boy next door had the best thoroughbred racer in the county, but we beat his pants off one Sunday. It was easy. I wouldn't run my nag over a third of a mile, and this boy was so anxious to show me up, he got sucked into the deal. The point being, make the other guy run *your* race.

"That's how we have to handle the Zeroes. Make 'em fight our fight. Take advantage of the few qualities in which the P-40 has an edge over the Jap fighter."

Chennault's strategy—later adopted by the U.S. Air Force when war broke out in December, 1941—was to avoid combat with the Zeroes unless the P-40's could take them by surprise from a superior altitude. His theory was that the heavier Tomahawks could attain sufficient speed in a power dive to make a single pass at the Zeros, then run away from them.

There was no sense in trying to dogfight with a faster, more agile craft when the odds were equal or you were outnumbered. If you could clobber them bad enough in that first pass so that the odds were on your side, then you might turn and fight it out. The Zero could always climb to safety beyond the ceiling of the P-40. But if the enemy chose to fight, Chennault felt, his pilots had to take advantage of the durability of the Tomahawk, which could take a lot of punishment and still fly.

"You'll never get a chance to latch onto the tails of one of those fast babies," he impressed on his men. "Meet 'em head on in a dogfight. Expect to get hit twice for every shot you get in. That's where the Achilles' heel of the Zero is. It only takes one good burst to knock off a wing or the tail."

The P-40 possessed another trait that was to give the men who flew it in China a "boost" that no mechanical advantage could ever provide. It had a pointed, sharklike nose with an air-intake scoop that approximated the recessed jaws of a shark.

On an inspiration, Chennault had his ground crews decorate all the P-40's with fiendish eyes, bloody tongues and rows of saw teeth along the edges of the air intakes. The result was a demoniac caricature of a tiger shark. The men of the AVG were not long in adopting the man-eating monster of the deep as their coat of arms. The "Flying Tigers" was born.

Pearl Harbor came before the AVG had a chance to get into action. The entrance of England into the war against Japan doubled Chennault's problems. Previously the Japs had been hampered by Burma's neutrality, and had to restrict their attacks on China's last lifeline to that part of the Burma Road that was in Chinese territory. Now they were free to blast the road along its whole seven-hundred-mile length and could strike directly at Rangoon, the port that supplied it, and at the rail lines ferrying goods for China from the port to the road's southern terminus.

The Flying Tigers went into action the day after Pearl Harbor, attacking an unescorted flight of ten Mitsubishi bombers over the Kunming strip. They racked up six kills and sent the survivors running for home with their tails between their legs. But this was nothing to get cocky about, Chennault warned them.

"Wait till you tangle with the Zeros!"

That moment came on December 20 when Chennault's relay stations flashed the word that an armada of bombers and fighters was headed for Rangoon to blast the precious supply of dumps and supply ships there.

"They must be intercepted at all costs," Chennault told Arvid Olson, commander of the 3rd Pursuit Squadron, "Hell's Angels," as the boys called themselves.

Olson nodded and grinned. "Five-to-one odds, eh? That's not so bad, Colonel."

It was a brilliant day with a clear sky and a blinding sun, that Christmas in 1941. An excellent day for a bombing raid, the Jap flight leader was congratulating himself; thinking, no doubt, that the cowardly American fliers would be running for cover as usual at the first throb of of a Zero engine. More likely, they would be gorging themselves on turkey, stuffing and pie in the gluttinous manner of all Americans on this most heathen of all their holidays.

It was the last thought that Jap commander ever entertained. For an instant later a 50-caliber shell tore through the cabin of his Mitsubishi twin-engine bomber and blew off his head.

Painted eyes flashing behind the whirring props, the licking tongues and bloody jaws leering ferociously at the foe, Hell's Angels came straight out of the red ball of the sun. The P-40's screamed in the wind as they dove on the formation of seventy-five bombers and thirty-five fighters with the big "red meatball" (the Rising Sun) insignia painted on their sides.

Employing Chennault's "two-plane element"—a leader, a wingman, with a third plane up and behind flying top cover—the Americans rammed through the heart of the Jap formation.

Arvid Olson never took his finger off the trigger as the first element hit the level of the Zeros. There was no need to sight; the Japs were jammed close together. His tracers found the cockpit of one Zero, killing the pilot, and it swan-dove out of the formation. A second Jap took it in the engine, and he, too, dropped out with flaming fuel spewing back toward the cockpit.

Then Olson was through on top of the bombers. His 50-calibers shattered the plexiglass bubble of a Mitsubishi's tail gunner. A tracer tore into another's gas tanks and the explosion cracked the ship in half. Olson's wingman literally cut the left wing engine off a third bomber, and it flipped over on its back and spun toward the ground.

"Don't look back, kids!" Olson radioed his boys, and held the Tomahawk in its dive as he burst out the bottom side of the Jap formation.

One by one the elements of the 3rd Pursuit Squadron hammered the Japs and outran the protecting Zeros in their long rocketing glides.

When it was over, nineteen Zero fighters were burning on the ground in addition to fourteen bombers. Leaderless and panicked by their 30 per cent losses and the ferocity of the terrible "tiger sharks," the remainder of the formation fled in confusion back to their bases.

For the first time in the ten-year-old Chinese-Japanese War, the proud Jap Air Force had taken a humiliating beating. Indeed, it was the closest thing the Allies could point to as a "victory" since the attack on Pearl Harbor.

For the next five months the Flying Tigers held the air over the Burma Road and kept the port of Rangoon open until the Japanese land forces captured it in 1942. Here are a few of the amazing exploits the Tigers performed: They shot down 299 Jap planes, plus an indeterminate number of probables (a twenty-to-one ratio); forty of its members qualified for acedom in that short period; and they killed ninety trained Japanese airmen for every Tiger pilot who was lost.

"My angels!" Madame Chiang Kai-shek referred to them. "With or without wings."

In April of 1942, the AVG was incorporated into the United States Air Force as the 23rd U.S. Fighter Group, part of the China Air Task Force. Chennault was recalled to active duty as a brigadier general and given command of the Task Force. The Flying Tigers designation stuck, however, as did the lurid tiger shark painting on the P-40's, and the Tigers went on to further glory under the combat leadership of Colonel Robert L. Scott.

Only five of the original AVG stayed with the 23rd though. The rest returned to the States and rejoined their old outfits in the Army, Navy or Marines.

7.

WHEN THE FLYING TIGERS broke up, Gregory Boyington was a qualified ace with six kills to his credit. Upon his return to the United States, he was quickly reinstated in the Marine Air Corps with the rank of major and, after a stint at San Diego, shipped out to the Pacific again. At Espíritu Santo, a small island in the New Hebrides, Boyington was put in command of a squadron escorting bombers and transport planes up the "Slot" in the Solomon Islands. It was uneventful duty, and he did not have any opportunity to improve on his combat record.

Then, just before his outfit was scheduled to get into some real action, Boyington, who describes himself at that time as "the biggest drunk in the Corps," got into a free-for-all that put him into a New Zealand hospital with his leg in a plaster cast. It looked like the end of the road for the old Tiger veteran.

By the time Boyington got back to Espíritu his outfit was long gone, and he was shoved into the dreaded replacement pool with an assortment of other disconsolate characters, rejects, misfits and sickness refugees like himself from bomber, fighter and transport squadrons.

Boyington was thirty-one years old—very old for a fighter pilot—and he had a game leg. The future seemed to hold nothing but paper work and other light duty which he detested. Then he had a brainstorm, and sold it to a sympathetic colonel. Boyington's idea was to form a new fighter squadron out of recruits from the pool, led by himself, of course.

In his great autobiography, *Baa Baa Black Sheep*, Boyington tells of the trials and tribulations he faced in selecting his group:

"I knew that most pilots wanted to be fighter pilots if they were dumb enough. . . . I'll never forget two SBD pilots who wanted to go with me so badly, but they didn't catch on very fast. About all one could say for them was that they were in the same sky with the squadron . . . but they were all guts."

The one bright note was that the Marines were now equipped with new Corsair fighters with powerful engines and triple props that made them a match for the vaunted Zeros.

Officially the squadron was designated 214, but Boyington's motley crew christened themselves "Boyington's Bastards," in honor of their dubious origin. And Major Boyington himself became "Pappy" to the youngsters, most of them under twenty-two years of age.

An imaginative ground crew sergeant with a talent for drawing designed the squadron insignia: a shield with a sketch of a woebegone-looking black sheep on its face and a long black bar bisecting the shield diagonally.

"What's that for?" Pappy asked curiously, pointing to the bar.

The sergeant grinned. "Don't you know nothing about ancient history? In the old days, a man advertised his illegitimacy by having the bar on his shield run in a diagonal instead of straight up and down."

Boyington turned to his boys. "Let that be a lesson to you guys. A man worth his salt should never be ashamed of his background."

The men of 214 got the message. Past performance was irrelevant in this big game of life and death. The only thing that would matter was what they did in the future.

The first mission was a big one: escorting 150 bombers down the "Slot" to clobber the Jap Solomon stronghold at Ballale.

Leading the twenty-plane Corsair formation that flew top cover, Pappy did a lot of thinking and praying. There was a low cloud ceiling over the target, and as luck would have it, he lost the bombers. Frantically, Pappy took the squadron down, trying to break through the clouds and find his charges. Abruptly they were through into the open, and *flying right in the middle of an enormous formation of Zero fighters!*

It took a while for both Americans and Japs to realize what had happened. One Jap pilot, Pappy recalls, actually grinned and waved as they flew wing tip to wing tip.

Pappy recovered first and flipped on his gun switch and electric sight with nervous fingers. The Corsair's six 50-calibers burped into action, and the incredulous Japs found themselves being sprayed with tracers.

The Zero directly ahead of him burst into flame and flipped into a dive.

"I'm with you, Pappy!" the radio crackled, and Boyington recognized the voice of his wingman, Moe Fisher.

Fisher's guns accounted for the plane which had been flying next to Pappy's victim.

"Just like the old shooting gallery at Coney Island," Fisher commented.

Now the last of the American bombers were completing their passes at the target.

"Bandits at three o'clock attacking our big friends!" Pappy shouted. He banked the Corsair into a sharp turn and dove at the Zeros. As the Corsair hurtled toward the enemy at full throttle, one of the Zeros veered to meet it in that precarious game of "chicken" that brought two planes racing toward each other at speeds in excess of 400 mph.

The Zero and the Corsair opened up on each other at the same time. A 20-mm. cannon shell arced gracefully over Boyington's canopy. He saw his 50's sweeping the Zero, but still it came on. It was too late to turn away now and Pappy knew it; he braced himself for the inevitable collision. Then with less than thirty yards separating the two ships, the Zero disintegrated—vaporized—in a flash of high-test gasoline and Pappy's Corsair flew straight through the hail of debris which shattered against his plane as a storm batters a small boat on the high seas.

The bombers were out of danger now and heading for home.

"I'm gonna hang around for a while, boys!" Pappy radioed his crew. "Always was the last one to leave a party."

A few minutes later he spotted a Zero flying back to base, hugging the wave tops in the manner of fighters who are out of gas or ammo and who want to escape detection. Pappy went into a power dive and came up fast on the Zero's tail.

Then, as his finger tightened on the trigger, he had a premonition. Swiveling his head, he saw a second Zero coming in fast on his tail from six o'clock. Pappy stood the Corsair on one wing and turned to meet the new foe. The Zero came on with its cannon and machine guns blasting. Luckily, the Corsair escaped any vital damage. Then, as the Zero pulled up to avoid a collision, Pappy rammed a burst of 50's into her exposed belly. The Jap lobbed over him and squatted in the water like a wounded duck.

By now Boyington's gas was low and he started home. Minutes later he saw one of his own boys down close to the water, looking real mushy. A Zero screamed out of nowhere and punished the helpless Marine, who seemed unable to take evasive action. Pappy raced to the rescue, but it was too late. Oil and flame shot back from the doomed Corsair's engine.

Furiously, Pappy latched onto the Zero's hind end and let go with everything he had in his guns. The Jap pilot pulled back hard on the stick and his maneuverable little ship nosed up at almost 90 degrees. Pappy tried to follow suit, but the heavier Corsair stalled and toppled over in a spin. But not before Boyington saw the Zero lose a wing.

He got the engine revved up just in time and flattened out several feet above the waves. That was enough for one day, he decided, and headed back for Espíritu.

There was a big reception committee waiting for him when he landed. Pappy was hoisted high on the shoulders of his "Bastards" and lugged around the field. To his surprise, he learned that he had accounted for three kills in the battle over Ballale. These, with the two he had just downed, gave him five for the day. *He had gone from ace to double ace in a single battle!*

The rest of the squadron hadn't been idle either. With Pappy's skein they had accounted for a total of thirty Jap planes.

Notoriety however, had its disadvantages. The big

brass complained that it was embarrassing to the American public to read the word "bastard" in print, as applied to their All-American boys doing battle in the Pacific. So Pappy had to find a new name for 214.

It wasn't very hard. The answer was there in the insignia—the black sheep.

"Actually it's even a better name," he told the boys. "We're the black sheep of the Corps, that's for sure."

And that is what it remained until the end: Boyington's Black Sheep.

By January of 1944, the Black Sheep were world-famous. Pappy himself was the nucleus of a contingent of newspaper reporters who dogged him every minute he was on the ground.

The reason behind their attention was that his personal combat record had, for two weeks, been poised on the brink of history. The all-time record for enemy planes destroyed in combat had been set by Captain Eddie Rickenbacker in World War I. Rick's record was twenty-six kills. Pappy was one behind, and he had as much trouble getting that one as Roger Maris had trying to equal the Babe's 60 homers in 154 games.

The squadron's second tour of duty was only days away; and all the Black Sheep knew that would spell the end of their combat careers. With almost 150 sure and probable kills to their credit, Washington would rule that the war was over for 214.

Pappy knew Washington was right. Malaria, fungus and 101 other miserable tropical diseases were ravaging the men. Boyington couldn't eat or sleep, and was riding the razor edge of battle fatigue. The magpie clamor of the reporters, *"When are you going to break the record, Major?"* didn't help.

Day after day, Pappy would patrol the skies, searching for Zeros; sometimes, he would fall asleep at the controls, and only awaken when the Corsair spun into a dive. He knew he was pushing his luck, that his reflexes were slow, that his skill was gone, that whatever edge he had held over his Jap counterparts was slipping fast. But that magic figure was an obsession now: 27-27-27-27-27 —he saw it in his dreams, the magic number that would break the record. With only a few days remaining it seemed impossible.

On January 3, Boyington led a fighter patrol over Rabaul. As the formation approached the target, Zero interceptors rose to meet them. *It's now or never*, Pappy told himself, and throwing caution to the winds he raced his Corsair into a steep dive to meet the enemy.

Captain George Ashmun followed him down yelling, "I'm covering you, Pappy! Give 'em hell!"

Overeager, Boyington blazed away at four hundred yards, too far away to aim accurately. But the old luck was back with him again—briefly. His burst caught a Zero in the engine and his heart leaped as lovely flame ringed the cowling.

"You got it! You got it!" Ashmun crowed.

Then they were in the midst of the gaggle of Japs, both firing wildly. Ashmun scored a hit. Boyington had only an impression of "round wing tips and square tips" painting the blue sky in a whirling, surrealistic montage. And "those horrible Rising Sun markings!"

And finally it happened: one of the "meatballs" flashed into his sights. Pappy fired a burst and it hit dead center. The Jap rolled and nosed down.

"You made it!" Ashmun shouted over the radio. "You broke the record. Number twenty-seven, Pappy."

"Let's get the hell out of here!" Boyington told him, and shoved the power on full.

He pulled away from the Japs, but Ashmun was in a bind, with five Japs on his tail.

"Dive, George!" Pappy pleaded, but Ashmun was having trouble with his Corsair.

Pappy banked and turned toward the battle again. His Corsair came on fast, but the Japs were pouring it into the crippled Ashmun fiendishly now, and Boyington knew his wingman would never make it home as oil whipped back in the slipstream of his prop. There was still a chance if he could belly-land the crippled ship in the water or bail out. But Pappy had to get those Japs off his tail first.

Forgetting his own safety, Pappy hurtled into the middle of the Zeros, his 50's spitting. He kicked the rudder back and forth, wobbling the Corsair from side to side, so that the tracers played back and forth over the enemy ships the way a stream of water from a moving hose plays over a lawn.

A Zero exploded into flame. Number twenty-eight! But it didn't make any difference somehow. Ashmun's plane dove out of control and he did not eject. The cockpit was all aflame.

Pappy fought back the tears of sorrow he always felt at the backs of his eyes when one of his boys got it, and broke away from the Zeros. His belly contracted as tracers drifted past his left wing. Two more Zeros were on his tail.

He rolled, dove, jinxed the Corsair every way he knew how, but he could not shake them. Slugs shattered the instruments on the panel, and Pappy felt the sting of a Jap 7.7 in his thigh. Then the whole cockpit seemed to explode with a roar. A direct hit by a 20-mm. shell under the seat! Blood filled his flying boot.

So this is how it is! Pappy thought with grim humor. *This is how it is to be on the receiving end of the stuff that records are made of.*

The Corsair was burning now, still hurtling down with breakneck speed. Flames were licking all over the canopy now as the high-test gas sprayed over the cockpit. No use trying to bail out, he knew. He'd be burned to a cinder before he hit the water.

You finally got it, wise guy!

There was one chance in a million. He loosened his safety belt, then threw the stick forward as far as it would go. The Corsair nosed down and bucked like a bronco. Pappy hurtled head first through the canopy and flames like a man being shot out of a cannon. His chute caught with a jerk that almost tore his arms out of their sockets. Almost instantly he hit the water.

Pappy got out of his chute harness and swam to the surface. The angry Japs made several strafing passes at him, and for five bad minutes Pappy, submerged a few feet beneath the surface, watched with bursting lungs as the Zero 7.7's scaled and hopped across the surface above him. He was almost ready to give it all up, when his Black Sheep came to the rescue and drove off the Japs.

With his strength ebbing fast from loss of blood—his leg was broken from the 20-mm. shell that had exploded in the cockpit; there was a slug in his other leg; and his torso was perforated with shrapnel—Pappy inflated his rubber life raft and hauled himself aboard. Collapsed in the bottom of the raft, he waved as the Black Sheep buzzed him, saluting with their wing tips.

Then, one by one, they turned and headed back for Espíritu. He watched with a calm sadness as they became dots on the horizon, then disappeared. Pappy and the boys both were well aware that this was "good-bye." Barring a miracle, Colonel Gregory Boyington would go down in the record books as the "bastard who died breaking Eddie Rickenbacker's record."

That is exactly how it happened, too. The Black Sheep did not see Pappy again. A grateful nation mourned for a brave Marine hero. And the President presented his parents with the Congressional Medal of Honor.

Over a year later, the world learned that Lady Luck

had not abandoned her favorite Black Sheep. The same day he had been shot down, a Jap submarine had picked him out of the Pacific. Pappy was held in a PW camp in Japan, where he had to sweat out the rest of the war in monotony—and safety.

8.

"WE WERE Johnny-come-latelies," an ex-Black Sheep recently told a reporter. "And we had a ship that could keep up with the Zero in a dogfight. The guys who really deserve most of the credit were the guys of VMF 121. They held the line at Guadalcanal in the bad days of 1942 and '43 when the Japs outclassed us and outnumbered us in the air. No, sir, the Japs will never forget Joe Foss and his Flying Circus."

Captain Joe Foss had spent his first year of war as a stateside training officer. This was the time when the bright young military psychologists were insisting that a man started to go downhill after the age of twenty-one years and only the sharpest youngsters could qualify for fighter pilots. Joe Foss, a Dakota farm boy, was twenty-seven, so the Marine Air Corps brass simply ignored his incessant pleas for combat duty. Then the Solomon campaign bogged down, and the Corps began to suffer from a shortage of competent twenty-one-year old pilots. So "old Joe" got his chance at last.

In September, 1942, Captain Foss stepped off a transport onto Guadalcanal. At Henderson Field he was assigned to Squadron 121 and given command of two flights, eight planes. The Marine pilots had plenty of guts, but morale was not of the highest. Joe was dismayed to discover that the Zero was held in positive awe.

"It can outclimb a homesick angel," one lad told him gloomily.

Henderson Field resembled a piece of terrain on the moon with its profusion of bomb craters from around-the-clock Japanese bombing, and the handful of Grumman Wildcats on the island were helpless to stop them.

Joe Foss knew the first thing he had to do was to whip confidence into his squadron. As Chennault had minimized the inferiority of his P-40's by concentrating on their strong points, so Foss "sold" the Wildcat to the Marine pilots.

"Hell, the Grumman can absorb its weight in lead and still keep fighting. How would you like to be one of those poor Jap pilots in that *papier-mâché* Zero? No protection at all."

He stressed the hit-and-run tactic that the Flying Tigers had used so successfully against the Zeros in China. Then Joe really showed his genius—the military psychologists could have taken some pointers—by introducing the spirit of competition into his group. He divided the eight pilots into two flights made up of "The Farm Boys" and "The City Slickers." Together they were known as "Joe Foss' Flying Circus."

Almost from the time Joe took over, the Jap superiority in numbers and equipment was offset by that priceless quality known as *esprit de corps*. But it took more than "heart" to stop the Japs.

Huddled in their foxholes, the Marines read week-old newspapers that proclaimed: "MARINES ON GUADALCANAL DOOMED!" And it was easy to believe as the forces of Nippon hammered at the American lines night and day, on the ground and from the air. Malaria and jungle rot inflicted more casualties than Jap lead.

Supplies were dwindling—at one time there was less than a hundred gallons of aviation fuel on the whole island! And on top of everything else there were the incessant, torrential rains. It seemed inevitable that Henderson Field would fall to the Japs. Then, without any air support, it would be only a matter of time before American forces were pushed off the island completely.

On Sunday, October 25, one of the largest attack groups of Zero fighters and Mitsubishi bombers clobbered Henderson Field. With bombs exploding all around them and Jap fighters strafing the field, Joe and his men struggled frantically to dig their Wildcats out of hub-deep mud and take off. It took almost a full hour to put five planes into the air.

The outnumbered Wildcats had one advantage: The sky was thick with clouds. A wild game of hide-and-seek progressed all through that morning and into afternoon, as wave after wave of Japs came over.

All of the men of the Flying Circus were superb that day, and Joe Foss was the most phenomenal of all. Most pilots consider themselves lucky to have perfect 20-20 vision. Foss had 10-20 vision, which means his eyes were twice as sharp as those of the normal man. His reflexes matched his vision.

Conventionally, the surest method of shooting down an enemy in a dogfight is to "get on his tail" and fire from a six-o'clock position, where you can keep him in the sights. At high speeds, kills made from the three o'clock or nine o'clock slots (deflection shots) are extremely rare, and lucky.

That Sunday as Joe's Wildcat was still climbing, a Zero flashed across his nose at a right angle, a mere blur in the overcast. A single burst from the Wildcat's 50-calibers punctured the "meatball" insignia and sent the Jap crashing in flames. Then a Zero was on his tail and scored a direct hit on one of his engines.

Joe scooted into a cloud and took stock of the damage. The hit engine was damaged beyond hope, so he feathered it. Only a damned fool would have gone out look-ing for a fight with one engine gone. But when Joe saw one of his Country Boys diving with two Zeros on his tail, he unhesitatingly left the safety of the cloud cover and went to the rescue. On one engine it was mushy go-ing, and there was no hope of overtaking the Zeros and latching onto the classic six o'clock position. Instead Joe cut across their direction to try for another deflection shot. Once again those amazing eyes and reflexes were true. The Zero closest to the fleeing Wildcat exploded in the air, and the second one veered off in another di-rection.

Having taken the pressure off his "chick," Joe squatted on the pock-marked strip like a mother hen. Without a word to anyone, he leaped from the plane and raced to another that was being revved up for take-off.

"Knock those blocks away!" he yelled to the ground crew. And with a roar of the twin engines, he was in the air again.

Nine Zeros screamed down on top of him. But now there were six Wildcats to cover their leader, and they blasted three of the Japs out of the sky and flushed the others away.

The cat-and-mouse game resumed, with Joe and his boys dodging in and out of the clouds to blast away at the bombers and fighters. One Zero followed Foss into the "soup" and there commenced a weird blind dogfight. Under these conditions Joe's uncanny eyesight gave him a decided advantage and he notched his third kill of the day.

Meanwhile, the Country Boys and the City Slickers were outdoing each other to pile up their respective scores. Finally, with twenty-two of their bombers and fighters burning in the steaming jungle, the Japs decided they had had enough of the Flying Circus for one day. On the ground the soldiers leaped out of their foxholes and began to shout and whistle at the sky as the Japs ran for home.

In shooting down five enemy planes that day, Joe Foss brought his score up to seventeen. More important, that battle signified the shift of the balance of air power on Guadalcanal. From that time on it would be all downhill for the Japanese. Their stranglehold had been broken.

Less spectacular was another air "battle" fought over Henderson Field that same month in which no single shot was fired, but actually it was an even greater victory for Joe's Flying Circus.

The alert was sounded for what was estimated to be the biggest strike the Jap Air Force had ever directed at Henderson Field—well over a hundred planes. Foss and the Marine Air Commander knew that the combined strength of Squadron 121 could not hope to turn back a formation like that no matter how much better their pilots were.

But Joe, the amateur psychologist, had a gimmick up his sleeve. "I'll go upstairs with my boys. The rest of the squadron stays on the ground."

"You're out of your mind!" the squadron leader protested. "You won't stand a chance."

"Not in a fight, we won't," he admitted. "But if I know my Japs, maybe we won't have to fight."

At the briefing he gave his City Slickers and Country Boys astonishing orders.

"All we're gonna do is fly back and forth across the field at about five thousand feet. No matter what happens, you are not to break formation or fire your guns."

"What are we gonna do?" one pilot asked. "Commit suicide and get it over with real quick like?"

"We're sitting ducks, all right," Joe admitted, "if the Nips jump us. I'm counting on the perverse Oriental mind to pull this one out of the fire."

The Flying Circus was obedient to Foss' seemingly mad plan. And when the advance fighters approached the field, they saw eight Wildcats flying back and forth across the field in a neat holding pattern that was positively mouth-watering. All they had to do was dive and *bang! bang! bang!*

But wait! What were the tricky Americans up to? The Zero fighter squadron leader was very familiar with the pugnacious qualities of the Flying Circus crew. And their present behavior was decidedly unnatural. He told his pilots to stand off while he and his wingman went down to investigate. Diving in a split-S the Zeros came within a hundred yards of the patrolling Wildcats.

"It was almost more than we could bear," one of the Country Boys recalls. "One time I had this Zero right in my sights, but I kept my finger off the trigger."

After about five minutes of futilely trying to draw the Wildcats into a fight, the Jap squadron leader went upstairs and rejoined his squadron.

"This must be a trap," he radioed his pilots, as well as the group leader of the oncoming bombers. "Those Americans are trying to lure us down, and then scores of fighters will drop out of the clouds and destroy us."

Convinced that the unorthodox behavior of Foss' boys concealed some horrendous pitfall, the vast Jap armada swung about and returned to base without dropping a single bomb or firing one shot. Once again Joe Foss had saved the day.

On January 25, 1943, four months after Foss had arrived on Guadalcanal, the Flying Circus terminated its brilliant tour of duty. The final score stood at forty-two kills for the Farm Boys and thirty for the City Slickers, which, as one of the Farm Boys put it, "destroys for all time that myth about us hayseeds buying gold bricks and the Brooklyn Bridge."

As for Joe himself, he went back to the U.S. and received the Congressional Medal of Honor from Franklin D. Roosevelt personally for: "a record of aerial combat achievement unsurpassed in this war . . . undaunted by tremendously superior numbers. . . . His remarkable flying skill, inspiring leadership and indomitable fighting spirit were distinctive factors in the defense of . . . Guadalcanal."

Joe Foss' leadership was not a fleeting thing inspired by love of combat and patriotism. In 1953, he was elected Governor of South Dakota by an overwhelming majority, and proved himself to be as bold and courageous on the political front as he was on the battlefront.

Of all the aces who fought in World War II—in the Pacific or the European Theaters—none had such a short, glorious career as "Butcher Bob" Hanson, barely twenty years old when he joined the Marine's vaunted 215 Squadron in the Solomons in November, 1943.

In six missions over Rabaul, the key Jap fortress in the Solomon Islands, First Lieutenant Hanson destroyed twenty-five Jap planes—twenty of them within seventeen days!

His real moment of glory came on an escort mission for U.S. B-17's bombing Empress Augusta Bay during a Marine amphibious landing. At the height of the landing, Hanson spotted six Jap torpedo bombers skimming across the water toward helpless transports. Peeling away from his squadron, he intercepted the enemy planes before they could drop their torpedoes.

On his first pass he scored a direct hit on one of the torpedoes slung under the carriage of the lead plane. The explosion disintegrated the bomber and sent the others swerving away from the ships.

Hanson was after them like a cat after mice, raking

all five with 50-calibers. Fearing they would suffer the fate of the first bomber, the others finally jettisoned their torpedoes and scooted back to their bases.

Now Hanson turned his attention to a flight of American bombers that were being harassed by Zero fighters. So intent were the Japs on their lumbering victims that they were unaware of Hanson's presence until he was in their midst. His first burst set fire to the engine of the Zero on the tail end of the line.

Pouring it onto the American bombers, the Japs were reluctant to break off the attack because of one measly Wildcat. The Jap leader ordered his wingman to break away and engage the Marine fighter. As it went into its steep climb, intending to Immelmann and come back down on Hanson's tail, Butcher Bob anticipated the maneuver, and his nose pointed up a fraction before the Jap's did. He splattered it with 50's as it came spread-eagled into his sights.

Immediately he was on the heels of the remaining three Zeros. With his ammo running low, he conserved it by firing short bursts. A third Zero flamed out of formation. Then, as the last two realized the true threat this wildman presented and broke to the right and left, he caught one with the final slugs in his magazine. The last Jap wanted no part of the fiend who had destroyed four of his buddies and fled for home. The bombers—thanks to Hanson—all reached their bases safely.

For his remarkable contribution to the successful landings at Augusta Bay, Lieutenant Hanson was awarded the Congressional Medal of Honor. Sadly, before the tribute became official Hanson was killed in a daring strafing raid on Rabaul—not in aerial combat, as every good ace wants to go, but from a chance shot from a Japanese rifleman on the ground.

"Ironic," a buddy of Butcher Bob's commented. "All the aces in the Jap Air Force couldn't hang one on Bob.

It had to be some infantryman who probably couldn't hit a cow in the ass with a snow shovel. Bet he wore thick glasses, too."

But in the summing up it matters little how and why a man is killed in combat—in the sky, in the mud or in the deep blue ocean. Heroism knows no caste barriers—or reasons.

In the official statement appended to Robert Hanson's Medal of Honor the government acknowledges: "A medal seems so great an award, yet so little for a nation to offer to its young men who give their lives . . ."

9.

IN THE MATTER of publicity, our Navy pilots took a back seat in World War II. There are several reasons why this is true, none of them having anything to do with the quality of the naval air arm.

First of all, the Navy Air Corps was (and is) much more closely integrated with the parent service as compared with the Marine Air Corps and the Army Air Force of World War II. Naval pilots operated principally from aircraft carriers in the Pacific; they were dependent on navy personnel for care and maintenance of their planes; they lived, ate and associated only with the sailors.

Also, the monastic life aboard ship isolated them from contact with the public and press. But if the Army and the Marines monopolized headlines, the aces of the Navy carried the air war to the enemy with equal ferocity and drama.

No pilot in any service had about him more drama —or glamour—than Commander David McCampbell, boss of the "Fabled Fifteen," Air Group 15 flying off the carrier *Essex*.

The "Fabled Fifteen" was in the thick of all the big battles of the Pacific: the Marianas "Turkey Shoot"; Saipan; the Battle of the Philippine Sea; and the Battle of Leyte Gulf. In a rugged eight months of combat it amassed a record unequaled by any other Navy or Marine squadron:

    662 enemy planes destroyed
    400 probables
      3 enemy carriers sunk
      1 enemy battleship sunk
      2 enemy cruisers sunk
      2 destroyers sunk

        And badly damaged:
      1 carrier
      3 battleships
      8 cruisers
     20 destroyers

Naturally, some of these vessels were clobbered in concert with other squadrons.

With a record like that it is difficult to point to any single action which stands out from the total picture. But if there is one, that one must be the performance of the Fabled Fifteen during the critical Battle of Leyte Gulf on October 24-25 in 1944.

On October 20 of that year, MacArthur had invaded the Philippines. His forces had established a firm beachhead on Leyte, but the issue was still in doubt. Leyte Gulf was cluttered with transports and support vessels, vulnerable as the fish in the proverbial rain barrel—*if* the enemy could get to them.

Protecting the gulf on the north was Admiral "Bull" Halsey's powerful Third Fleet. To the south were the lesser forces of Admiral Kincaid and Admiral Clendorf. Together they comprised an armada that could repulse any attack the declining Japanese Navy could muster.

But the wily Japs did not intend to meet the Americans on those terms. Admiral Kurita conceived a daring and brilliant plan. A fleet of line ships steamed down the east coast of Luzon with much fanfare in the direction of Leyte Gulf, reckoning wisely that Halsey would construe this to be the last-ditch Jap offensive against the American Navy. Halsey snapped at the bait and ordered the Third Fleet to proceed northward.

With Halsey's major power drawn out of position, two other Jap fleets, proceeding from the Sulu Sea, closed a neat pincers on the lighter forces of Olendorf and Kincaid composed of outmoded, reconditioned battlewagons, light carriers and cruisers.

One Jap task force slipped in behind Halsey through the straits of San Bernardino and steamed down the east coast of Leyte; the other came down the west coast toward the straits of Surigao. The idea was to rendezvous at Leyte Gulf and devastate the troops and supply transports supporting the invasion. It almost succeeded.

Two factors saved the day for the Americans: the brilliant defensive battles waged by Kincaid and Olendorf in defending the Gulf with their outgunned ships and the magnificent performance of the Navy pilots.

On October 24, as he steamed north to meet the Jap decoy fleet, Halsey received word from his recon planes that a Jap naval force was threading the Bernardino Straits. Immediately he dispatched carrier-based fighters and bombers to strike at this force while continuing to head north.

This air group strike was so effective that it forced the Japs to turn back through the straits. Later that night, they reversed course again and made it through to the east coast of Leyte undetected, but minus their prize capital ship, the *Musashi*, whose 18-inch guns might have been decisive in the battle that took place the next day.

Worse than the loss of the *Musashi*, though, was the fact that the critical timing of the attack had been disrupted.

Instead of attacking simultaneously at either end of the gulf, the two Jap fleets attacked hours apart, relieving the American naval forces in the gulf of the disastrous necessity of splitting their fighting ships to meet the pincer threat.

Meanwhile, Halsey had received an urgent appeal from Admiral Kincaid to send reinforcements back to Leyte Gulf. By this time, he suspected that the Jap force off Cape Engano in the north was a decoy. Still, he hated to let such an easy mark off the hook. Old "Bull" had the temperament of a Las Vegas gambler. A firm believer that you "*can* have your cake and eat it too," he ordered his air arm to proceed north and engage the decoy fleet while his Third Fleet raced back to Leyte Gulf.

Here, too, the Navy's pilots covered themselves with glory. The Jap decoy fleet was virtually without any air support, as every available plane had been sent south to join in the coordinated air-sea attack on the invasion fleet in Leyte Gulf. Wave after wave of Grumman Wildcats pasted them, and when it was over four aircraft carriers, three destroyers and one cruiser, flying the Rising Sun flag from their masts, were burning and sinking in the warm waters of the Philippine Sea.

Meanwhile, the battle inside the gulf was gradually swinging in the Japs' favor. Kincaid's light escort carriers and destroyers put themselves staunchly between the heavy Jap task force off Tacloban and the transports and barges in the harbor. But such a fight could only have one outcome. Two American destroyers were blasted out of the water by the big guns of the battleships and the umbrella of Mitsubishi bombers and Zero fighters that covered them. Then an American heavy cruiser keeled over and sank.

The climax was strictly from Hollywood, however.

Just as it appeared as if the Japs might bring off their grand coup and doom the Philippine invasion, Bull Halsey's big fleet came steaming over the horizon, as it were, and the Jap commander Admiral Kurita knew that unless he ran, and ran fast, he would be the prey of an American counterpincer movement.

He broke off the attack and steamed back through the straits the same way he had come. The Battle of Leyte Gulf was over, and the Americans held the field—by the grace of God and the Navy pilots.

No group of warriors played a more vital role in any victory than did the Navy fighter pilots in the key Battle of Leyte Gulf. They battered the Jap fleet off Cape Engano. Their initial strike at Kurita's force sneaking through the Bernardino Straits upset the Jap timetable and robbed them of the use of their most powerful battleship, the *Musashi*. Even more important was the battle they fought to protect the ships in the gulf as hordes of Jap bombers and fighters attacked in conjunction with the Jap fleets.

In the thick of the fighting was Commander David McCampbell and his "Fabled Fifteen."

McCampbell and six mates were patrolling the Philippine Sea off the east coast of Leyte when his radio crackled.

"Look at that flock of bandits, ten o'clock low," his wingman, Lieutenant Roy Rushing, announced.

McCampbell whistled. "Must be a hundred of 'em."

There were, in fact, sixty Jap planes in the formation: twenty Mitsubishi bombers with a top cover of forty Zeros.

"What we oughta do is pretend we didn't see them," one of the boys cracked.

"Yeah," said another. "Only a bunch of damned fools would jump a bunch like that with the odds better than eight to one."

"You're so right," McCampbell agreed drily. "Okay, guys, let's go and get 'em!"

"Check!"

"Double check!"

The other six pilots all agreed enthusiastically.

Then, one by one, the Wildcats peeled off to the left and rolled over in the hawklike split-S dive to the attack.

"Roy," McCampbell told his wingman, "you and I'll stay upstairs and see what those Zeros are going to do."

Predictably, the Jap fighters dove to the defense of their bombers. Midway in their pass the first flight of four Zeros were intercepted by McCampbell and Rushing. McCampbell came in at five o'clock and shattered the leader like a clay pigeon. Rushing got another.

Both were well aware that they were exposing themselves to the remaining eighteen Jap fighters. But they poured on the throttle and dove through the bomber formation, each picking off one of the clumsy Mitsubishis as the heavy Grumman Wildcats augmented engine power with gravity to outrun the pursuing Zeros.

The Japs did not chase them for long; turning instead back to their bombers. A mile away the Wildcats reformed again and appraised the situation. The Japs' reluctance to fight could mean only one thing.

"They're land-based bombers," McCampbell said. "Looks like they're on their way to Manila."

It was no secret that the Japanese High Command was shuttling every available plane—land-based and carrier-based—to the Philippines to build up their air power for a massive strike at MacArthur's invasion fleet.

"Guess they have orders not to tarry and play games," Rushing suggested.

"And no Jap ever disobeyed an order," McCampbell said with shrewd insight into the orderly mind of the Jap military man. On this assumption, he led his small flight of Wildcats after the retreating Jap armada.

The seven Wildcats climbed above the Jap formation once more and trailed them for ninety minutes, snapping at their heels whenever the opportunity arose.

One of the Mitsubishi bombers developed engine trouble and fell behind. McCampbell was on it like a hungry wolf after a straggling sheep. A burst into the fuel tank finished it off. Number three of the day!

Two of the Zeros circled back to protect their charge. The Wildcats fell upon them viciously, and they joined the bomber in the drink.

The men of the "Fabled Fifteen" reassembled and flashed the thumbs-up sign to each other. Again they closed in on the Jap formation. As McCampbell had surmised, the Zero fighters did not attempt any coordinated offensive against their inferior-numbered foes. It did not occur to them to disobey—or deviate—from their orders to get to Manila as soon as possible.

McCampbell and his boys kept pecking away at them, making quick passes through the formation and diving away at high speed to safety. The commander got himself a fourth, then a fifth kill. And, as yet, the seven Wildcats were unharmed.

At one point a flight of four Zeros, their pilots frustrated beyond all patience, broke out of the formation and climbed vertically at the "Fabled Fifteen" bunch with machine guns and 20-mm. cannon flashing from their wing tips.

The Wildcats met them head on, returning the fire. Both sides scored hits, but the durable Wildcats could take superhuman punishment. Three of the Japs spiraled into the water, and Commander Campbell racked up number six for himself.

"It was a slaughter," one of the "Fabled Fifteen" recalls. "We cut those poor bastards to pieces. I bet there wasn't one Zero or Mitsubishi in the whole shebang that didn't have a slug or two in it."

Over Manila Bay Commander McCampbell shot down his ninth Jap plane of the engagement. Then, with ground fire bursting in deadly puffs all around them, the seven Wildcats, short on ammo and gas, climbed and ran for home.

No pilot in any service in any war in any air force has ever matched officially the record that Commander David McCampbell established that day the 24th day of October. Nine planes—almost enough to make a double ace in one flight! In addition, his mates claim that he may have killed a half-dozen others which, at last sight, were smoking and acting dangerously mushy.

For that feat, and for the vital deterrent it afflicted on the Jap air forces attacking the invasion fleet in Leyte Gulf, Commander David McCampbell was awarded a Congressional Medal of Honor, presented personally by the President at the White House in January, 1945.

Coming on top of his D.F.C. with two gold stars, his Navy Cross, Legion of Merit, Silver Star and Air Medal, the Medal of Honor did not evoke any immodest re-action from the shy Scotsman.

"Aw, what the heck!" he laughed. "I'm just a victim of circumstances. I'm a group commander. It isn't my job to shoot down planes. But the damned fools just flew into my sight, and what else could I do?"

Commander McCampbell did more than his share to win the Battle of the Pacific.

10.

OFFICIALLY THE FIRST American air group to see action in World War II was the Fifth Air Force—then General MacArthur's Far East Air Force stationed in the Philippines.

Three days after Pearl Harbor the Fifth Air Force

made headlines with the dramatic story of Captain Colin Kelly, Jr., who, according to the newspapers and commentators, had put his B-17 Flying Fortress bomber into a suicide dive down the smokestack of a Japanese battleship.

It was only after the war that the American public found out this story was a fabrication; many people, indeed, still believe the legend. In those black days of 1941 all America wanted—desperately needed—a hero. They *believed* in Colin Kelly, the way children believe in Santa Claus.

This is no apology for Captain Kelly. He needs none, for even though he did not sink a Japanese battleship, he was one of the war's first and great heroes.

In a lone B-17 bomber, Kelly slipped through cordons of Zero fighters covering a Jap naval flotilla, and made a pass at a heavy cruiser. None of his bombs hit the mark. Then with close to a dozen Zeros blasting him from all sides, Kelly flew his B-17 back to Clark Field in the Philippines. Over the field he ordered his three-man crew:

"Bail out!"

"What about you, Colin?"

"I'll be okay." The captain fought the almost useless controls. Smoke filled the cabin. The engine was leaking oil and coughing. The fuselage and wings were tattered from Jap 7.7 slugs and 20-mm. cannon shells.

Kelly stayed at the controls while his men wriggled out of the escape hatch. The smoke was blinding and choking him. Fire licked at his pant legs and hands. But he stayed until the rest of the crew were safely jettisoned. By that time it was too late to save himself. And Colin Kelly died—a true hero.

One-man offensives were a common thing in the Fifth Air Force in the first days of the war. The day after Colin Kelly was killed, Lieutenant Boyd "Buzz" Wagner set out to avenge him. Wagner was jockeying a P-40 Tomahawk fighter. His target was the Jap air strip at Aparri.

Officially, Buzz was on a recon mission, but when he spied the thirteen Zero fighters lined up in a row on the field, he couldn't pass up the opportunity. The P-40 roared across the field in a tornado of dust and gunfire, sending the Jap mechanics scattering in all directions.

As he pulled up again, Buzz turned and saw fire licking at two of the Zeros. He saw something else, not so pleasant—two airborne Zeros diving out of the sun at six o'clock. Buzz gunned his engine and kept down close to the deck where his P-40 engine had maximum efficiency. But the speedy Japs closed in fast. Buzz knew he had had it, unless he could pull a miracle out of his hat.

On a wild chance he cut his throttle suddenly, and the heavy P-40 lost speed rapidly, settling back on its tail. The faster, lighter Zeros, caught by surprise, broke right and left to avoid colliding with him and went sailing past the P-40. Buzz kicked the engine back to life and waggled the Tomahawk's nose from side to side spraying the Japs with 50-calibers. One burst into flame. The other lost a wing. Both crashed in the jungle.

Buzz rolled the P-40 in an Immelmann and came back across the field, strafing the grounded planes once more. This time he set fire to three more.

So far his score was three kills in the air and five on the ground.

His gas gauge was way down now, so he climbed and headed back for Clark Field. Halfway there, he spotted three more Zeros returning from a foray of their own. The sun was at his back so he had the advantage of surprise.

Diving, he met them head on, his tracers reaching out for them. *Bam!* One flamer! He lifted the P-40's nose and the stream of 50's caught a second Zero in the engine. Both planes spun into the seas, as Buzz continued on through the third and poured on the gas.

He landed safely with a day's record of ten Zeros destroyed: five in the air and five on the ground.

It was the Fifth Air Force that produced the two greatest American aces of World War II: Major Richard Bong and Major Thomas McGuire.

Dick Bong got off to a rather inauspicious start at Hamilton Field, outside of San Francisco, California. One morning in January, 1942, General George Kenney, Commanding Officer of the Fourth Air Force, received a report from the civil authorities in San Francisco that bulged his eyeballs.

"Get Lieutenant Bong over here at once!" he ordered an aide.

Second Lieutenant Richard Bong, twenty-one, dark, lithe and handsome, reported and saluted smartly. He was a little pale.

General Kenney pounded the report on his desk. "Lieutenant Bong, it is my understanding that you were flying a P-38 in the vicinity of San Francisco yesterday. Is this correct?"

Bong swallowed hard. "Yes, sir."

"And is it correct that you did a loop-the-loop around the Golden Gate Bridge, causing drivers to abandon their cars, thereby snarling traffic for two hours?"

Bong seemed to grow smaller. "Yes, sir."

Kenney's face got redder and redder. "And then did you buzz a group of young ladies who were eating lunch in the park?"

Bong's voice was weak. "I waved to them, I guess." As an afterthought: "I thought I rocognized one of the girls, sir!"

Kenney gripped the edge of his desk, fighting for control. "Lieutenant Bong," he said in a rasping voice, "you are grounded, mister, until further notice!"

That hurt, and Bong could not hide it. Flying was an obsession with him. "How long might that be, sir?" he asked in a tremulous voice.

"Maybe for the duration of the war!" Kenney roared. "Now get out of here!"

Soon after General Kenney was ordered to Australia to command General MacArthur's Fifth Air Force, he checked off three dozen names on the Fourth Air Force roster.

"I want these men transferred with me," he told his adjutant. "They have the real stuff."

Lieutenant Richard Bong was at the top of the list.

Dick Bong was what is known in the prize ring as a "workmanlike fighter." With him dogfighting was not a game; it was a science. There was none of the bravura, glamour and sparkle of the Boyingtons, the Cochrans, the Fosses about Bong. Shooting down Japs was a serious job, and he applied himself to his job as studiously as an engineer or a lab technician.

He averaged about one kill every five missions and his score rose steadily to twenty-eight, a new record for the USAF. Recognizing his rare scholarly approach to dogfighting, a subject to which the average ace had extreme difficulty attaching a "handle" for benefit of student pilots— *You just have to feel it*—General Kenney sent Bong back to the States as an instructor.

Now a major, Bong translated the intangibles of aerial combat into theorems which the novice could master:

"Defense against Jap fighters is resolved around superior speed of our fighters. If you are jumped from above, dive to pick up an indicated air speed of 350 mph, then level out and start a shallow climb at high air speed.

"If a Jap fighter does follow you in a high-speed dive, a 90-degree turn to the right will lose him. The Zero's controls stiffen . . . in a high-speed dive, and he cannot follow a high-speed turn. . . .

"An indicated air speed of never less than 250 mph is good life insurance in combat.

"Offensive measures . . . are always hit and run, because the Jap can outmaneuver us about two to one. Any number may be attacked from above. Dive on the group, pick a definite target and concentrate on it. . . . Pull up in a high-speed shallow climb and come back for another pass.

"Single enemy planes can be surprised from the rear and slightly below. . . . The Zero has a blind spot, and your first pass should knock him down.

"Against bombers it is safe to drive up right behind the tail, with the exception of the Betty and Helen. These two have 20-mm. cannon which cover a 30-degree arc to the rear, and a beam attack broken off before you reach this one is the best attack."

In October, 1944, after almost a year as an instructor, Major Bong convinced the Air Force that he could do a better job of teaching green pilots in the combat area than he could in the States. He had an ulterior motive.

Assigned to a forward base in New Guinea, Major Bong began "moonlighting" on the job. After hours he would tag along on missions to "see how my pupils are doing."

"That's not the way to do it, Joe," he would reprimand a new pilot over the radio. "Now let me show you."

And Major Bong's new Mustang fighter—the Zero's equal—would hurtle down into a gaggle of Jap fighters. Two bursts sent one flaming down into the jungle. Two more hung onto his tail like leeches. It looked like curtains for the old major, and his students groaned with despair as tracers piled into the tough Mustang.

Bong kicked the rudder and jinxed the ship, then shoved the ship forward. She climbed steeply, with the Japs following—but a beat behind. At the top of the loop he flipped her over and slid into a tight split-S that brought the P-51 onto the Zero's tails. Another quick burst killed one, and the other ran from the "master."

Back at the base Major Bong got a chewing out from his CO. "You had no business getting into that fight, goddamnit! Major, your job is instructing, and don't you forget it again."

"Yes, sir," Bong agreed pleasantly. "But you have to admit that demonstration is the best way to teach anybody anything."

Bong did forget the CO's admonition, time and time again. His lapse of memory helped the Fifth Air Force account for eight Zeros that never would have been downed if Major Bong—the instructor—had not indulged in his extracurricular activities.

In January, by direct order of Air Force Chief of Staff Hap Arnold, Major Bong was again returned to the States and placed, as it were, under wraps to keep him out of trouble. The war was over for the leading ace of the USAF, who had racked up forty kills in the Pacific.

The career of Dick Bong had an ironic, downbeat ending, the kind devotees of predestination point to and say: *Kismet*.

Just one week before the Japanese surrender in August, 1945, Dick Bong was testing the Air Force's newest fighter, the then revolutionary P-80 jet. The ship flamed out on take-off and crashed, killing Bong instantly.

Behind him he left a legacy of glory, a record of acedom not likely to be broken in any atomic war of the future, and every medal and award a soldier could win, including the Congressional Medal of Honor.

Significantly, Bong's Medal of Honor was not awarded for any single, dramatic, glorious action, but for the cumulative glory of a magnificent career.

11.

MAJOR THOMAS McGUIRE, second-highest scoring ace in the USAF with thirty-eight kills, had a singular dedication to teamwork that makes his combat record all the more remarkable. McGuire was not a lone-wolf seeker of glory, as were so many fighter pilots. And for that reason his exploits were submerged in the over-all brilliant performance of his squadron.

McGuire always stressed to his men the obligation of the individual to the group and the assigned mission:

"On escort missions, never let a Jap lure you out of formation into a personal scrap. . . . Our job is to protect the bombers.

"In squadron formation you not only have to think of yourself, but also of the fifteen men behind you (as a commander).

"In fighter combat, never break your formation into two-ship elements. Stay in pairs."

McGuire was the proverbial mother hen, always looking out for everyone else at his own expense. On Christmas Day, 1944, his squadron of P-38's flew top cover for B-17's raiding Mabalacat air strip. Over the target they were jumped by twenty Jap Zeros. The twin-engine Lightnings waded right into the Japs, tying them up while the bombers laid their eggs.

Major McGuire shot down one Jap, then spotted one of his boys under attack by three Zeros. Diving, he planted himself alongside the P-38, which was piloted by an inexperienced Lieutenant.

"Break right!" he ordered the other pilot. "Stand her on her nose and get the hell out of here."

While the other Lightning ran for safety, he enticed the Zeros to latch onto his tail. Riddled with 7.7's, he finally shook them, and maneuvered into a tight turn that gave him a deflection shot at his pursuers. One Zero went down and he chased the other until he flamed that one, too.

Now his guns jammed. But instead of getting out of the scrap like any sensible pilot, McGuire stayed right in the thick of the fray, radioing instructions to his team the way a football coach would, and feinting at Jap planes which threatened any of the Lightnings.

At one point, a P-38 was having extreme difficulty lining up a wily Zero for the kill. McGuire plunged down on top of the Jap and "held him still" while the American applied the *coup de grâce*.

The next day he led another escort mission over Clark Field, and, in another wild melee, scored four more kills. In this battle, too, McGuire narrowly escaped death when he lured four Zeros off the back of a crippled B-17. Outmaneuvering them, he then flamed two and sent the other two scooting for home. Seven kills in two days, bringing his total to thirty-eight. It would go no higher.

On January 7, leading a fighter sweep over Los Negros Island, his squadron encountered a single Jap Zero, and decided to have some fun and play a cat-and-mouse game with the Jap.

McGuire did not approve, but said nothing. There was no room for horseplay, he believed, when the stakes of the game were human lives. This day his worst premonitions were realized.

The Jap was brilliant—one of the brilliant Zero Pilots the American public never read about in the newspapers— and he evaded one, two, three, four flights of P-38's, feinted a single craft out of position and caught on its tail.

"Dive!" McGuire screamed into his mike.

The pilot obeyed, but the dive was too steep. He pulled up a mere hundred feet above the ceiling of the jungle. McGuire groaned. This was one of the green ones. Without climbing again, the Lightning went into rolls, banks and reverse turns which were made to order for the maneuverable Zero.

Without even taking time to jettison his bulky wing tanks—excess baggage, dangerous baggage in a dogfight—Major McGuire dove to the rescue. At treetop level he dueled with the Zero and shook it loose from his cub. Then, in a tight turn to shake the Zero off its tail, the overtaxed Lightning stalled, stood on her wing and plunged into the forest.

For his deeds of constant self-sacrifice, which ultimately led to his death, Major Thomas McGuire was awarded the Congressional Medal of Honor posthumously.

12.

ON PAPER the Thirteenth Air Force had one of the least spectacular records of World War II. Formed in 1943 to support the Navy and Marines in the Solomon Island campaign, the Thirteenth, at the war's end, could only boast twenty-seven aces, some of them enlisted crewmen, and her top-ranking ace, Colonel Robert Westbrook, just reached twenty kills.

To the Thirteenth Air Force, however—and namely to an inconspicuous captain named Tom Lanphier who barely achieved acedom with six kills—fell one of the most spectacular missions of the entire war.

It began in Washington, D.C. at an emergency midnight meeting between President Franklin D. Roosevelt and the Secretary of the Navy, Frank Knox.

"Naval intelligence has intercepted and broken a coded communiqué from Tokyo to the Jap commander in the Solomons," Knox told the President. "On April 18, Admiral Isoroku Yamamoto is scheduled to make an inspection tour of the front."

F.D.R. was wide-awake now. "Anything more specific than that?"

"We've got it pinpointed. Yamamoto will be flying over Ballale at precisely 1000 hours."

The President looked skeptical. "It must be some kind of a trick. Japanese top security can't be that lax."

Knox snubbed his cigarette out in an ashtray on the chief executive's desk. "The point is, can we afford to pass it up—even if it's only one chance in a thousand?"

Roosevelt brought the palms of both hands down hard on the green desk blotter. "No! You're right, Frank. We have got to assume it's on the level. You pass the word to Nat Twining: *Get Yamamoto!*"

Isoroku Yamamoto was Number Two man in Japan's military dictatorship—the man who had planned and executed the sneak attack on Pearl Harbor!

Eighteen new P-38 Lightnings were groomed for "Operation Revenge" until their twin engines purred like sleeping kittens. Their pilots were hand-picked for qualities of keen eyesight, quick reflexes, marksmanship and coolness under stress. This was to be no ordinary dogfight.

"The point is," Major John Mitchell, the group leader, briefed his seventeen pilots, "we won't get a chance to make more than one pass at Yamamoto's plane. They could have up to two hundred Zeros covering him."

"What it is, is an aerial ambush," a lieutenant ventured.

"Exactly," Mitchell agreed. "We've got to strike like lightning."

The men laughed nervously.

"That's what we're flying—Lightning," one man quipped in reference to the P-38's.

"We go in fast," said Mitchell. "And we get out fast!"

"We *hope* we get out," someone added.

Mitchell looked at him wryly. "You want a safe job, we can arrange to get you a desk in the HQ."

"When do we take off, sir?" the man said hastily.

"Tomorrow morning 0700 hours . . . Here's how we'll work it. Loose formation at 25,000 feet until we spot our target—*if* we spot it. Now get this! There will be only four ships in the attack section." He nodded toward a lanky, sandy-haired captain. "Tom Lanphier is the attack leader. . . . Tom, you boys will make the actual pass at Yamamoto's transport. The rest of us will run interference, keep his top cover busy."

Lanphier grinned. "I didn't really want to vote in the next election anyway."

"This one is going to be by the seat of the pants all the way," Mitchell told them. "No radio contact, no radar, nothing the Japs might pick up . . . All right, any questions?"

"Yeah," somebody cracked, "when does the first boat leave for San Francisco, Major?"

They all laughed.

"Okay," Mitchell dismissed them. "Lights out early tonight, boys."

On the morning of April 18, 1943, Major Mitchell's squadron was cruising 450 miles northwest of Henderson Field a few minutes before ten o'clock. The skies were empty.

As the minute hands of his wristwatch climbed to twelve and then past the one, Captain Tom Lanphier felt the tension drain out of muscles and nerve endings keyed up by twenty-four hours of expectation. Depression and disappointment, the natural aftermath of anticlimax, made his legs and arms leaden weights.

Then his eyes picked out the speck on the horizon. He glanced out of the canopy toward Mitchell's plane. The leader's P-38 was waggling its wings frantically, the prearranged signal in the absence of radio contact.

According to plan, Captain Lanphier led his attack group into cloud cover while Mitchell and the other thirteen pilots climbed at full throttle to decoy the Zeros covering the Jap admiral's Mitsubishi transport.

Adrenalin poured through Lanphier's veins now, and the lassitude of a few moments earlier was gone. Through a break in the cloud cover, he caught a glimpse of the approaching Mitsubishi. Mitchell and his group had drawn off most of the covering Zeros, but there were still a formidable number of Jap fighters boxing in the admiral's plane.

Lanphier and his wingman, Lieutenant Rex Barber, jettisoned their empty fuel tanks in preparation for the strike. Lanphier's belly lurched as he watched Lieutenant Besbey Holmes bucking his P-38 like a bronco to shake loose his tanks, but the mechanism that released them had jammed!

With those tanks Holmes would be handicapped in combat much in the manner of a guy playing tennis with a full field pack strapped to his back. A sitting duck! Lanphier made his decision. Breaking the radio silence, he ordered: "Bes, you stay upstairs!" To Holmes' wingman, Lieutenant Hind: "Ray, you cover him."

Then, with his attack force halved, Captain Lanphier shoved the throttle all the way forward and the P-38 surged out of the clouds with an impetus that pressed him hard against the leather back rest. Barber was a half-length behind him.

The air speed indicator climbed past 450 as Lanphier

dove at the Mitsubishi from ten o'clock position. The Zeros saw them now, and kicked out their fuel tanks.

A flight of four Japs flying wing to wing came at the two P-38's, with another group of three right behind.

We'll never make it! Lanphier thought, and flipped on his gun switches. The Zeros and the Lightnings raced head on toward each other, while the Mitsubishi, with Yamamoto aboard, banked away toward the jungle, Lanphier flew through a hail of tracers, marveling that he was not being hit. His own machine guns and cannon were blazing back at the Japs. A thrill raced down his backbone as one of the Zeros took a direct hit from the P-38's cannons and exploded. Lanphier threaded the Lightning through the gap in the formation left by the destroyed Zero, and the rest of the Zeros went racing by him, skidding on their tails as they tried to turn tight.

The bomber was racing across the treetops about a mile away now, trying to make the field at Kahili before the P-38's could get at her. Barber had taken on the second flight of Zeros singlehanded, so there was nothing between Lanphier and the fleeing bomber.

Lanphier banked and dove at high speed for the Mitsubishi, with the Zeros after him. The powerful Lightning outdistanced them, but as Lanphier pulled up on the Mitsubishi's tail, her tail cannon began to blast away at him, too close for comfort. Wasting precious time, he banked to the right and came around in a wide turn that brought him in at two o'clock, with his sights leading the bomber.

This was a precarious maneuver. To avoid overshooting her, he cut back on the throttle and brought the Lightning's nose up to brake his speed. The indicator fell rapidly to 250. Both the bomber and the P-38 were so low now that the top branches of the trees were tearing chips and splinters off their bellies. If either pilot made the slightest miscalculation, it was *finis!* And the P-38 was getting down to stall-out speed.

At the same time, the Zeros were closing on Lanphier from nine o'clock. It was still anybody's game, a fifty-fifty chance that the Zeros would get Lanphier before he got the bomber.

Lanphier let go with all his guns, jerking the nose of the P-38 up and down so that his tracers followed a serpentine path across the bomber's nose, the way a child's jump rope snakes up and down in little waves when one end is flipped. The most common mistake a fighter pilot makes in attempting a deflection shot is undershooting or overshooting a fast-moving target. Lanphier's tactic allowed for this common misjudgment.

Goddamnit! He almost shouted for joy as the right engine burst into flame.

Lanphier had accomplished the mission. The plight of the Mitsubishi was hopeless. But his own predicament was almost as bad as the P-38 settled back on its tail and threatened to stall out. Lanphier coaxed the twin engines along and fought for altitude.

The event reminded him of a scene in a slow-motion movie sequence. The burning bomber floated past him and he cruised slowly toward the deadly barrage her rear gunner was throwing astern of the stricken Mitsubishi. There was no room to duck under her out of the cannon's range, and the bomber's cannon commanded a 30-degree arc above her tail. At the same time the angry Zeros was converging on him.

But the *grande dame* who decides the fate of all men was with Captain Tom Lanphier that day. Just as it seemed inevitable he would fly straight into the cannon barrage, the bomber hooked a wing on a tall tree and cartwheeled into the jungle with a belch of fire and smoke.

There were still the Zeros to reckon with though, and

they were all over the P-38, raking her with shell and machine guns. Straight ahead loomed the Kahili air strip where a dozen more Jap fighters were taxiing to take off. Lanphier gunned the Lightning across the field at an altitude of fifty feet, almost ramming one Zero as it left the ground and causing a string of others to abort their take-offs.

In the dust and confusion, he lost the Zeros which were on his tail and climbed over the harbor. The powerful torque of the twin props took hold now, and Lanphier climbed in a high-speed bank. To the east he caught up with Major Mitchell and the rest of the squadron, re-grouping after their fight with the other fighters. Climbing away from the demoralized Japs at Kahili, they headed east—and home.

In a great war, one cannot attach undue importance to personalities and single episodes of valor. But if it can be said that any one man deserved a lion's share of the credit for "avenging" Pearl Harbor, that man would have to be Captain Tom Lanphier. For he, personally, fired the shots that destroyed Admiral Yamamoto, villain of the infamous December attack on Hawaii, and perhaps the guiding genius of Japan's war machine.

13.

THROUGHOUT World War II, U.S. newspapers and other communication media fostered the impression among the American public that the Japanese aviators were a tribe of subhuman grinning little men with buck teeth and thick bifocal spectacles. This myth may have been comforting to the public, but it elicited only bitter snorts from the men who had tasted the accuracy of Jap bombardiers at Pearl Harbor and who fought them in the air over The Philippines, the Solomons, Midway,

New Guinea, Iwo Jima and the other Pacific monuments of the biggest war in history.

At the beginning of the war, no nation in the world set such stiff requirements, mental and physical, for its air cadets as did the Imperial Japanese Navy. These were the pilots who flew the vaunted Zero, and they flew it with a skill and vengeance unmatched by any other air service. The record of the aces of the Japanese Navy speaks for itself:

Naval Air Pilot First Class (NAP 1/C) Hiroyoshi Nishizawa racked up 104 official kills before he was killed; NAP 1/C Shoichi Sugita claimed 120 plus; Ensign Saburo Sakai, 65 accredited kills; Lieutenant Naoishi Kanno, 53; NAP 1/C Matsumaro, 50 plus; Commander Tadashi Nakajima stopped counting at 75.

In 1942 and 1943 these pilots were benefited by the superior numbers and superior performance of their fighters, but with the emergence of the American P-38's, P-47's, P-51's and the Grumman Wildcat, Hellcat and the Corsair, the Zero and the Japanese Naval Air Force lost control of the Pacific skyways. It was during this critical phase of the war, in late 1944 and 1945, that the aforementioned Jap aces proved their true mettle.

Saburo Sakai, blinded and crippled in the dogfight that netted him his sixtieth kill, was grounded permanently in 1944 and assigned to light duty. But when U.S. forces thundered back to the Philippines and pounded at Japan's front door at Iwo Jima, Sakai demanded to be reinstated. Although he was still blind in one eye and his body and nerves were ravaged by malaria and fever, the High Command accepted his services. These were desperate moments, days of crisis.

None of his squadron mates gave Sakai much of a chance to survive his new assignment with the Yokasuka Air Wing. It looked as if they were right, too, when, on his first mission Sakai became separated from the squadron and was jumped by fifteen Grumman Hellcats. The Hellcat was faster than the Zero and had a much higher ceiling. All it had to do was make a quick pass, then climb out of reach again until another opening presented itself.

These fifteen Hellcat pilots decided to play cat-and-mouse with the lone Jap before they finished him. Sakai found himself pinned in the center of a ring of swirling Hellcats. He tried to dive under them and climb over them, but they anticipated his every maneuver and blocked it. His only hope was to reach home base at Iwo Jima where he could duck into the cover of Japanese antiaircraft fire, but that was a forlorn hope. Iwo was not even visible on the horizon.

At last they tired of the game and came at him like hungry sharks slashing at a victim in the sea. Sakai had been experiencing a bad case of the shakes up to this point. His hands were clammy, his fingers stiff with tension, his belly squirming with butterflies.

Like a green recruit! he thought with disgust.

With the first clatter of gunfire, it left him. A flight of four Hellcats were coming in at six o'clock, their wing guns twinkling. Tracers arced across the Zero's tail and wings. All the skills and experience of five years of dogfighting in China and all over the Pacific could not be erased by fever, a blind eye and fatigue. It was almost as if some external force were manipulating Sakai's hands, feet and reflexes.

He spun the Zero on its left wing in a fantastic tight turn, and the Hellcats were firing into thin air. A second flight came at him, and once again Saburo Sakai shook off the faster planes. This time he spun onto the last Hellcat's tail and sprayed it with 7.7 slugs. The flight scattered and climbed to safety.

Sakai was mad now, and he darted here and there like a giant darning needle feinting at one enemy plane after another, guns and cannon blazing. The Hellcats fled to a safer altitude and regrouped while Sakai gunned his Zero in the direction of Iwo.

He didn't get very far before the Americans overtook him again. Now it began once more—the grim game of tag at twenty thousand feet above the Pacific Ocean. Rolling, turning, diving and feinting, Sakai shook off the Hellcats the way a star quarterback shakes off tacklers. It was a breath-taking display of aerial "broken-field running."

Now the battle was almost on top of Iwo Jima. On the ground mechanics and Jap pilots watched with awe as the man everyone thought was finished forever did things with a Zero no one of them had ever seen done before. The contrails from its exhaust painted pretzel designs in the sky as it eluded the Hellcats time and time again.

Although Sakai had no opportunity to get in a burst of 7.7's steady enough to down any of the sturdy enemy ships, he did put several out of the action. Few of them escaped one or two holes in wing or fuselage.

Finally, he swooped down over the field beneath the protective umbrella of ack-ack thrown up by the Japanese gun batteries. Tracers arced up from all sides of the strip, covering the Zero and driving the Americans off. When Sakai landed, he was literally dragged from the ship by hysterical squadron mates and pounded on the back until he almost collapsed.

Commander Nakajima threw his arms around Sakai's neck and there were tears in his eyes.

"Hey, cut it out!" Sakai said gruffly. "You'd think this was my funeral."

Nakajima shook his head and smiled. "No funeral. Today I saw a man reborn. Maybe some of it will rub off on the rest of us."

But time was running out, and the Japanese would learn the bitter lesson the Americans had learned almost four years earlier at Pearl Harbor and on Bataan: All the spirit and valor in the world cannot stem the tide of superior numbers in a modern war.

Two last-ditch efforts to forestall the inevitable were put forth by the Japanese Air Force.

On October 24, NAP 1/C Hiroyoshi Nishizawa led a history-making mission during the Second Battle of the Philippine Sea in the early days of the American invasion of the Philippines—the first of the dreaded *Kamikaze* attacks.

Literally, *Kamikaze* means "the divine wind." In 1281, when the Chinese Emperor Kublai Khan sent an invasion fleet against the Japanese mainland, certain disaster was averted when a great storm blew up without warning and drove the warships away from Japan, piling them up on the rocky Chinese coast. The religious Japanese attributed their last-minute reprieve to their gods, who they imagined had stirred up the "divine wind."

In 1944, when the Japanese High Command began to accept the fact that they could not win the Pacific War, Admiral Takijiro Onishi conceived the idea of a "suicide" corps which would be composed of fast planes carrying big bombs or torpedoes. Their pilots—mainly green recruits who were expendable—would dive the planes with their explosive cargoes directly into vital spots of major warships of the American fleet, thus eliminating the miscalculations inherent in ordinary bombing attacks.

Zero fighters manned by the best pilots in the Japanese Air Force would fly cover for these *Kamikaze* planes, so named in honor of the "divine wind" which had saved Japan from the conqueror centuries before.

Nishizawa led the flight of Zeros which covered the first *Kamikaze* strike on the warships crammed into Leyte Gulf in support of MacArthur's invasion transports.

The suicide planes themselves were commanded by

Lieutenant Lukio Seki. They were second-string Zeros, each carrying a massive bomb.

The grim procession took off from Clark Field outside of Manila just before dawn on October 24, 1944. Rain was falling, and thunderheads rolled through the sky like tumbleweed, their undersides lit up by sheet lightning. The Zeros bucked and skittered about in the turbulence the way leaves do in a gale. Nishizawa had his hands full keeping his group together.

At last, after battling the storm for almost an hour, they broke through the overcast as the gray light of the new day filtered bleakly over the choppy sea. Five miles away, Nishizawa could see the dim shapes of the American fleet barely discernible against the dark water.

He issued a final reminder to the pilots of the covering Zeros: "Remember, we must stay together. Each of you will fly wingman for one of the *Kamikaze* ships. Under no circumstances will you break formation to engage in personal dogfights until the mission has been accomplished. The *Kamikazes* must get through even if it means letting ourselves get shot down."

Then to his friend Lieutenant Seki of the *Kamikaze* flight: "Good luck and—good-bye."

Throttles wide-open, the ten Zeros screamed out of the clouds and down on top of the fleet. Simultaneously a gaggle of Hellcats raced to head them off. The air was saturated with the dark plumes of ack-ack. Tracers zigzagged in all directions. A U.S. Navy Grumman tried to sneak through the outer ring of Zeros to get at the *Kamikazes*. Nishizawa kicked his rudder and let go with all his guns and cannon, throwing up a steel wall between the Hellcat and the suicide plane it was trying to nail. The Hellcat veered off.

Now another Hellcat was on Nishizawa's tail. He held his course, instead of making the obvious tight turn the

Zero was so adept at. Tracers bracketed his wings. The sensation of helplessness was terrible. He jinxed the Zero, rolling and trying to feint the Hellcat out of position. Fortunately her pilot was overeager, and none of his shots struck a vital area.

As the ships loomed up directly ahead, Nishizawa became oblivious to his own danger. Breathlessly, he watched the *Kamikaze* piloted by Lieutenant Seki dive on a big carrier. Straight as a dart it went through a maze of tracers sent up by the vessel's frantic gunners.

Miraculously, it got through, and then it hit! A great ball of fire devoured the little Zero as it exploded against the superstructure of the carrier. The shock wave hurled Nishizawa's ship high into the air, when it seemed as if he, too, would not clear the mast of the carrier. He pulled back on the stick, the spell broken, and climbed away fast.

He looked down and back of him. Another *Kamikaze* crashed onto the deck of the same carrier. This one broke through to the magazine. A chain of explosions literally broke the big carrier in two. She rolled on her side and began to sink.

Nishizawa turned fast as he climbed, intending to rejoin any of his mates who were in trouble. But the whole thing was over before he could make a second pass on the fleet.

He saw a *Kamikaze* strike on the bridge of a heavy cruiser.

The fourth one in the string exploded in mid-air as a Hellcat blasted it barely a hundred feet from its target.

The fifth plane scored a direct hit on a light cruiser, and in minutes the ship was a floating pyre for all aboard.

Nishizawa climbed into the clouds with the other Zero escorts behind him. It had been phenomenally successful, this first *Kamikaze* raid. A carrier and a cruiser definitely sunk; another cruiser badly damaged. His escort flight was all intact. In spite of the success, Nishizawa felt no elation.

It was one thing for a warrior to die in fair battle with a worthy foe, no matter how great the odds against him, a battle where he had *some* chance of emerging victorious and alive. But there was something so coldly pagan and inhuman about these suicide attacks, in which there was not one sporting chance in a million of a man coming back alive. Japan's greatest air ace, Hiroyoshi Nishizawa, felt a little sick to his stomach.

The *Kamikaze* Special Attack Corps scored other spectacular—if fanatic—successes against the American Fleet off the Philippines and particularly during the bitterly resisted invasion of Okinawa. But there was little glory to be derived from these sorties because they were motivated by vengeance without any real hope of victory; motivated by the same vindictive, destructive impulse that led Adolph Hitler to sacrifice thousands of German lives uselessly in the final death throes of Nazism.

The final—and true—epic of glory and courage was written by the aces of the Japanese Naval Air Corps who were rallied from all parts of the crumbling empire in the last six months of war to form an elite fighter wing on Skikoku Island. The Matsuyama Wing was made up of men like Sakai, Nakajima, Sugita, Matsumara, Muto —all the best.

It was the Matsuyama Wing that introduced the new Shiden Japanese fighter plane into combat. The Shiden was the Jap's answer to the Hellcat and the Corsair, a sturdy plane that could climb and run with the American planes, and still outmaneuver them in close combat; its four wing cannons were more than a match for the firepower and armament of the Corsair of the Hellcat.

In its debut it badly bloodied the nose of a superior formation of attacking Hellcats. In his memorable book,

Samurai, written in collaboration with U.S. military expert and writer, Martin Caidan, Saburo Sakai relates vividly how he watched that battle from the ground because of a shortage of fighter planes.

Sugita was magnificent. Singlehanded he pounced on a flight of Hellcats in a vertical dive. One burst of his wing cannons splattered a well-armored Hellcat as if it were made of balsa wood. Sugita yanked back on the stick and the remarkable Shiden skidded and made the quickest recovery any of the American pilots had ever seen. A second cannon volley blew off a Hellcat's tail and rudder assembly, and it went down like a rock.

The remaining two tried to run, but the Shiden pulled up on their tails with ease. This time, Sugita polished off his victim with a machine-gun burst. The last Hellcat escaped into a cloud bank, and Sugita gunned the Shiden back to where his squadron mates were having a field day.

As Sakai describes it: "Every man on the ground cheered and shouted as one Hellcat after another went down. This time it was different . . . this time the Americans fought for their lives."

Before the decimated Hellcat formation fled in disorder for home, Sugita had notched his seventh kill of the day, the best day of a Japanese ace during the war.

That night, as the aces of the Matsuyama Wing toasted each other in the mess hall, hope flared briefly beneath their tunics. But there were too few Shidens, too few Sugitas. And even the best fighter pilots cannot beat the odds of the game forever.

One month after his finest hour, Shoichi Sugita was killed when he tried to take off during an American raid on his base. A Corsair fighter caught him with a burst when his wheels were barely off the ground, and the Shiden flipped over and exploded.

One by one they all met the fate of the fighter pilot

who pushes Lady Luck too hard: Kanno, Muto, Nishi-zawa, the men who rank with the international aces of all time. Though their cause may have been ignoble, the manner in which they defended it can only deserve the respect of all men everywhere who honor valiance and courage.

PART FOUR

The Battle of Europe

14.

THE UNITED STATES Eighth Air Force was the work horse of the Allied war machine in Europe. Its speciality was strategic daylight bombing which the Royal Air Force had abandoned early in the war because it was "suicidal."

The *Luftwaffe*, smarting under the hammer blows dealt out to it by the RAF in the mass daylight raids during the Battle of Britain, concurred, and when the Eighth Air Force arrived in England in the spring of 1943 and announced its intention of operating by daylight, Hitler and Göring were overjoyed. Here was an opportunity to avenge the defeat suffered by the *Luftwaffe* in the great raids over England in 1941.

The pioneer missions flown by the Eighth did not discourage the Nazis' elation. Extravagant losses marked those early efforts. In a single raid on the German ball-bearing plant at Schweinfurt, the Eighth lost 60 bombers and over 600 crewmen; 130 planes were badly damaged.

In the raid on the Messerschmitt factory at Regensburg, German fighters shot down 60 more and damaged 148 bombers. One of the first daylight raids on Berlin cost the Eighth 80 planes and 700 men. It began to look as if the British and German experts were right: Daylight bombing was just not practical.

U.S. Air Force brass refused to accept this. Daylight bombing was infinitely more practical than blind night raids because you could pinpoint targets, they insisted.

What made them so costly was the lack of adequate long-distance fighter protection. U.S. fighter escorts in 1943 simply did not have the range to accompany the big bombers deep inside Germany. The upshot was that the bombers customarily completed the final leg of their mission without fighter cover so that they were at the mercy of the ME-109's and FW-190's. The answer to successful daylight bombing had to be found on the drawing boards of America's aeronautical engineers.

The engineers and designers met the challenge with the development of the P-38 Lightning and the P-51 Mustang. When these fighters began to arrive in quantity in England, the Eighth Air Force went on a rampage that paralyzed German industry, disrupted transportation throughout Hitler's "European Fortress," strangled the *Luftwaffe* and paved the way for the Allied invasion of France in June, 1944.

It is a truism of the U.S. Air Force that no plane is any better than the man who flies it. The men who flew the P-47's, the P-51's and the P-38's over Europe and Germany were the best in the world. In two years of war, the fifteen fighter groups of the Eighth Air Force *destroyed more than nine thousand enemy planes* and produced *eight of the twelve leading aces* of all the United States Air Forces.

The Eighth's top ace was Colonel John C. Meyer of the 352nd Fighter Wing. Colonel Meyer, flying a Mustang, accounted for thirty-seven Nazi fighters and bombers. All of his air battles were spectacular. Once he and his wingman waded into a formation of twenty German fighters and knocked down five before scattering them.

On another occasion Meyer took on fifteen all by himself and flamed four. The greater the odds against him, the fiercer Johnny Meyer became.

But of all his fights the one that, perhaps, is the most

memorable for Colonel Meyer is the one that took place on New Year's Day in 1945.

Just a month earlier, American newspapers were featuring headlines suggesting the European War would be over by Christmas. Allied armies were racing toward the German border unopposed. Patton's Third had cracked the Siegfried Line. The *Luftwaffe* had practically disappeared from the air. What did the Germans have left to stop the Allied victory drive?

What the Germans had was Von Rundstedt, thirty crack divisions and a reserve of fighters and bombers that Herman Göring had been covertly building up for months. On December 16 Von Rundstedt launched his Ardennes offensive, to become historically famous as the "Battle of the Bulge."

For two bloody suspenseful weeks, the outcome of the German breakthrough teetered this way and that way. If the point of the Nazi offensive could not be contained, disaster would overtake the Allies. They might even be pushed back into the English Channel with enormous losses of men and equipment, which could prolong the war indefinitely.

At the height of the crisis, Colonel Meyer's 352nd Fighter Group was ordered to the battle front to support the badly harassed Ninth Tactical Air Force working in cooperation with the ground forces. This was a new line of work for the escort pilots.

"But it all amounts to the same thing," observed one veteran. "Shooting down Nazis."

The 352nd was based at Asch, Belgium, in the sector where *Luftwaffe* fighters hammered most persistently at U.S. supply dumps and communication lines. One of the group's three squadrons was airborne during all of the daylight hours, and the American aces fattened up their scores considerably during this period.

On December 25, Colonel Meyer, the Deputy Group

Commander under Colonel James Mayden got himself three ME-109's for a "Christmas present" to lift his total to thirty-two—tops for European aces at that time.

On New Year's Eve, Colonel Mayden assembled Meyer and the squadron commanders for a briefing.

"Call off all patrols for tomorrow," he advised them. "The whole group will be flying cover for a bombing mission into Germany."

Meyer frowned. "Helluva time to pull us off the line. Who's going to mind the store while we're over Germany?"

Mayden shrugged. "I'll just keep my fingers crossed."

"I don't like it," Meyer said. "Maybe we can at least fly a patrol in advance of the mission. Can you imagine what will happen if the Jerries get a lead on this? They could sit up above the clouds until the group starts taking off and BAM! No more 352nd!"

Mayden looked pained. "I'm with you, Johnny. But we have our orders. No patrols tomorrow."

Colonel Meyer couldn't sleep that night. A premonition hung over him like a shroud. In the battle zone, you had to borrow from the infantry. No sane infantry outfit would jump off on a big mission without sending out scouting patrols to feel out the enemy. Yet that was exactly what the 352nd was going to do the next day. Forty-eight Mustangs would be all lined up on the strip tomorrow neat as ten pins. No cover above them. Nothing! What a situation for an enemy ambush!

In the distance he could hear church bells ringing in the New Year. Pistol shots and *ya-hoos* sounded all over the areas. A dark form appeared in the entrance of his tent and whispered: "Colonel, how about joining us in a drink?"

Meyer pretended to be asleep.

Next morning he rolled out of his blankets before it was light, a firm resolve in his mind. At group HQ he got permission from Mayden to phone Ninth Air Force. He requested a change in the orders.

"For security reasons we'd like to hold back one squadron from that escort mission," he told the commanding general's office."

"General Quesada won't hear of it," was the reply. "This bombing mission needs maximum fighter support."

Meyer, a persuasive speaker, would not accept the decision unless it came from the general personally. An irate Quesada got on the phone. After lengthy discussion, the general agreed to compromise. Two full squadrons, plus four Mustangs from Colonel Meyer's squadron, the 487th, would fly the mission. Meyer would lead his remaining twelve Mustangs on advance patrol.

At 100 hours, the morning fog began to burn off the field, and Meyer and his crew climbed aboard their idling Mustangs. The colonel was anxious to get off. The sight of all those transport and fighter planes cluttering up the terrain—waiting to take off on the escort mission—made him uneasy. He glanced up at the overcast. No one could tell what was lurking up there.

Tension eased as he got the green light from the control tower and taxied to the head of the runway. The P-51's engine came to life with a ferocious roar as he advanced the throttle. The Mustang leaped ahead with the spirit of its namesake.

His wheels had cleared the ground when he saw them: A long line of FW-190's hedge-hopping across the rolling green countryside straight ahead. At the same time he heard the squawk in his headset:

"Bandits! At twelve o'clock . . . and three o'clock . . . and—hell! They're everywhere!"

There is no time even to retract his landing gear. No speed or altitude to take any evasive action. The only thing Meyer can do is hold course and climb—and pray.

He flips on the gun switches and electric gunsight just as the Nazi FW's clear the edge of the field.

This is a "showdown," aerial version. He must "shoot from the hip" the way the old Western marshals did it. The Mustang and the lead 190 open up at the same moment, their tracers crossing in the fast-closing gap between them. One of Meyer's shells explode at the root of the FW's right wing. It seems as if they must collide now. Then, abruptly, the FW noses down and crashes, missing the straining Mustang by a whisker. Meyer hears the rattle of flying debris on his underbelly. Now he is out of the battle zone, climbing.

At 2,500 feet he spots two 190's before they see him. He cuts in behind them as the Mustang gets her "air legs." The airfield is a madhouse. He holds his breath as his squadron mates take off through their own flack barrage spitting up from the antiaircraft guns on the edge of the field. The German planes with their distinctive noses and black crosses swirl over the scene like bats, strafing, bombing and turning all hell loose on the unmanned helpless planes parked on the field.

Meyer jockeys in behind the two unsuspecting FW's. His tracers rake "tail-end Charley." Then to his surprise, he sees tracers floating across his own wing. He glances back and notes with some surprise that an ME-109 is on his tail. He sees something else that almost makes him laugh. The ME pilot doesn't know it but he too is being tailed!

The "daisy chain" flashes across the field. Meyer throws a final burst at the FW ahead of him, then breaks sharply to the right to evade the ME. His slugs hit home, but the FW is not mortally wounded. The ME does not fare as well. At is goes by him, Meyer sees it flame as one of his Mustangs scores a hit on the fuel tank.

Colonel Meyer skids around, seeking another foe. No problem. The air is full of them. He gets on the tail of *another FW-190 and sticks with it through a series of panicky contortions by the Nazi pilot. Steadily he pumps shells into the wings and fuselage without seeming effect.*

He must have a rabbit's foot in his back pocket!

In a last desperate attempt to shake the Mustang, the German dives and leads Meyer through a heavy concentration of antiaircraft fire. It almost works! Flak tears at the Mustang's belly and rips a hole in one wing big enough to slip a watermelon through. But Colonel Meyer is determined to see this one out to the end. He pours round after round into the German. Just as they sweep over the far end of the field, his guns run dry. Meyer curses softly.

Abruptly the 190 wobbles and her engine spurts flame. The curse turns into a silent cheer. The pilot bellies down in a field, skims and bounces over the rough ground and, finally, flips onto her back.

His ammo gone, Colonel Meyer climbs out of the fight and watches his boys clean things up. And clean up they did! At 1·100 hours the Germans run for home, leaving twenty-three of their fighters burning junk heaps in the woods and meadows around Asch.

When Meyer landed his badly shot-up Mustang, he got a hero's welcome. If it had not been for his foresight, the Nazi fliers would have wiped out the American base and destroyed most of the aircraft on the field. As it was, they damaged a few buildings, shot up a few fighters and transports, and knocked down four fighters of Meyer's Red, White and Blue Squadron. But happily all the pilots were able to bail out safely. All thirty-six Mustangs assigned to the escort mission took off on schedule, and they made possible the paralyzing strike inflicted on Von Rundstedt's supply lines later that day.

And so Colonel Johnny Meyer and the 352nd took a place of honor alongside the "Battling Bastards of Bastogne"—General Patton's Third Army and all the other brave fighting men who blunted the Ardennes Salient and smashed the last Nazi offensive of World War II.

15.

Only slightly less bitter than the rivalry between Eighth Air Force fighter pilots and the *Luftwaffe* pilots was the intramural rivalry between the two leading groups of the British-based U.S. Air Force.

In two years in action, the 4th Group (The Wolfpack) and the 56th Group (The Debden Gangsters) each destroyed more than a thousand German planes, with the 4th holding an edge of about fifty kills. On the other hand, the 56th held a similar edge in actual air-to-air kills, and its own losses were only about half the losses of the 4th. Moreover, the Wolfpack numbered among its personnel four of the twelve top aces in U.S.A.F. history: Lieutenant Colonel Francis S. Gabreski, 37½ destroyed; Colonel David Schilling, 33 destroyed; Captain Robert S. Johnson, 28 destroyed; Major Walker Mahurin, 19½ destroyed (an additional 6½ in the Korean War for a total of 26).

Both the 4th and the 56th were blessed with colorful, fighting leaders. Colonel Hubert Zemke, CO of the Wolfpack, personally shot down nineteen enemy fighters and destroyed another seven on the ground; Colonel Donald Blakeslee, of the Debden Gangsters shot down fifteen and destroyed another two on the ground.

The 4th was the first to see action and had run up a commanding lead flying British Spitfires early in 1943. When the Eighth Air Force become totally operational, all groups flew P-47 Thunderbolts. The pilots of the 4th never did get the hang of the "seven-ton milk bottle" as they called the heavy, powerful P-47. The 56th loved it, and soon overtook and passed the Wolfpack.

Then, in 1944, the P-51 Mustang was introduced to the Eighth Air Force, and overwhelmingly adopted by the pilots of the 4th Group. The P-51 was lighter, sleeker, more maneuverable than the P-47, far more to the liking of the boys who had been weaned, as it were, on British Spits. By the end of the war the Wolfpack had regained their lead in group competition and they held it.

The exploits of the 4th and the 56th—all the fighter groups of the Eighth Air Force—would fill an encyclopedia. It is almost impossible to pick any single action and say: "This was the big one!"

To the pilots themselves, a major milestone in the air war in Europe was the first American bombing raid on Berlin. For eighteen months the Eighth Air Force had been pounding strategic targets in France, Belgium, Holland and the fringes of Germany, but up until March, 1944, the German capital had been immune to daylight bombing attacks. Hermann Göring bragged that no B-17's would ever penetrate the cordon of *Luftwaffe* which protected Berlin in the daylight hours.

As was mentioned earlier, the limited range of the American fighter planes enabled the fat air marshal of Germany to keep his promise for eighteen months. But with the emergence of the long-range P-51 Mustang and improved strategic techniques, the problems involved in bombing Berlin diminished. At last the moment arrived. On March 6, 1944, the Eighth Air Force would send eight hundred bombers to the German capitol.

Among the groups flying cover for the mission were Colonel Zemke's Wolfpack and Colonel Blakeslee's Gangsters.

That day the 56th had every available Thunderbolt in the air—seventy-two in all. They were split into two groups—A and B—of thirty-six planes each. Each group would rendezvous with a formation of a hundred B-17 Flying Fortresses over Holland and escort them to the target.

At 25,000 feet Johnson's Group B joins the "big friends" and splits into three squadrons, two flanking the tight boxes of bombers, and one on top cover.

Shortly after they cross into Germany, Johnson spots what appears to be a flock of birds coming over the southeast horizon. Gun switches are flicked on automatically. The pilots get set to jettison the belly tanks. The specks get bigger. They are not birds.

"Bandits at two o'clock!" Johnson shouts into the mike.

"We'll take care of 'em," Lieutenant Quirk of the 62nd Squadron assures Keyworth Red Leader Johnson. His twelve P-47's peel off from the bombers' right flank and race to intercept the blunt-nosed German 190's.

Johnson's fighter, All Hell, hits a bump and shakes itself like a nervous filly. He grins.

"You'd like to get a crack at those babies, too, wouldn't you, old girl?"

They are halfway to the target now. Johnson tries to pick up Group A on the radio. A cacophony of gunfire and voices crackles into the earphones.

"Mayday! Mayday!" an unfamiliar voice screams the distress signal. "We need help!" Then the radio goes dead.

Johnson is in a dilemma. No way of telling where the call came from. Static dominates all else as the German ground stations jam the air waves to cut communication between elements of the mission.

The group leader scans the horizon all around them. No sign of planes, German or American. Reluctantly, he orders the 63rd Squadron to make a scout to the north. With only twelve planes left to convoy the bombers,

Johnson takes the 61st Squadron up above the boxes of B-17's. They are approaching the point where the short-range P-47's will turn over their charges to the Mustangs which will go all the way to Berlin with the bombers.

The Eighth Air Force had worked out an elaborate system of relays, whereby the P-51's and the P-38's flew straight to rendezvous points, avoiding combat so as to conserve gas. Dogfights required rich fuel mixtures which rapidly depleted precious fuel—the P-47 drank a gallon of gas a minute at full throttle!

The hands of Johnson's wristwatch close rapidly at 1200 hours.

"Bandits at two o'clock!" *someone shouts.*

At least two dozen FW-190's are diving at the lead bombers. The twelve Thunderbolts race to intercept them, but too late.

"ME's at eleven o'clock!"

Johnson curses. Messerschmitts—maybe forty of them —are coming in from the other side.

"More of the bastards at twelve o'clock high!"

Over a hundred German fighters are converging on the B-17's from three directions. The B-17 gunners open up on the fighters, the tracers from their ten 50-caliber machine guns throwing a protective coating of lead around each plane.

The German and American fighters alike have equal hazards as they mix it up with the Fortresses' 50's flying all around them; the B-17 gunners find it impossible to distinguish between friend and foe as fighters flash by at top speed. Shells and rockets zip through the air into the B-17's. Their huge bodies tremble under the impact, but they stagger on like wounded mastodons. The FW's and the ME's are really pouring it into the tightly packed boxes of bombers.

Johnson is heartsick as one after another of the big friends drop out of formation and spiral earthward with smoke trailing in their wake. Some explode in mid-air, cremating their crews, but the sky is filled with scores of parachutes, as the majority of the crews escape from their stricken ships.

The Germans are hurting, too. Johnson sees two FW's collide in the in-fighting. An ME miscalculates on a pass at one B-17 and rams it amidships. The sky is a blue canvas and the pattern of the dogfight outdoes Picasso's maddest painting.

Johnson closes on the tails of two FW's. All Hell really breaks loose as her eight wing-guns spit fire. One of the Germans breaks up and chunks of flaming debris whip back into the Thunderbolt's prop.

He sights on the second FW when he gets the "May-day" distress call from his wingman. A Messerschmitt is hot after the wingman. Johnson slides the Thunderbolt to one side, losing speed and the P-47 and its pursuer race past him. He cuts in behind the ME and chases it away with a short burst.

Now Johnson and his wingman attack four FW's who are making passes at helpless Americans dangling from the ends of parachutes. The enemy planes scatter, but Johnson is after the leader, whose plane has the yellow nose reserved for top aces. He is set for a real fight this time.

As Johnson dives at him, the All Hell doing better than four hundred, the FW skids to one side, hoping the Thunderbolt will bull past him. Johnson anticipates the trick and cuts his throttle.

Now he'll cut left, he decides.

The Nazi does, spinning on one wing in a beautiful tight turn that would have lost the Thunderbolt under normal conditions. But Johnson is already turning into the turn before the FW breaks.

The FW passes through the circle of the P-47's gun-sight and Johnson squeezes the trigger. The enemy fighter trembles under the barrage of 50's that plaster it. The German ace dives steeply now, trying to outrun Johnson. But the P-47 plays this game better than any aircraft in existence. The ground rushes up as the FW fills up the sight. Taking his time, Johnson neatly carves a wing off the German with his guns. No time for the pilot to bail out. All Hell breaks up and is climbing as the impact of the explosion sends shock waves racing through the air.

Gas and ammo are low. The B-17's are out of sight, probably under the wing of the Mustangs by now. The Germans break off the fight and race after the bombers. Johnson is happy to see them go. He spots six P-47's circling above him, and joins them.

"Let's go home, boys," he orders.

"Roger."

The 61st heads back to England, as do other groups of two, three and four planes of the 56th Group. It has been a busy day for the Gangsters.

The party is not over yet for Colonel Zemke and his Wolfpack. They are part of the mission that must take the B-17's over Berlin and out again.

The one-two punch of the 4th Group is the team of Captain Don Gentile and Captain John Godfrey. Between them they accounted for some sixty-six German planes by the war's end. According to Hoyle, a wingman is a kind of aerial "straight man." He covers "his ace" in combat so that the lead man can concentrate on shooting down enemy planes. Wingmen, like good blockers in football games, rarely get their pictures in the paper.

The team of Gentile and Godfrey—appraised by former Air Chief of Staff Arnold as "the greatest in history"—had a different relationship. It was not uncommon for Gentile to hand the reins to his wingman in a battle and say: "You're in a better spot to get that baby than I am. I'll cover you. Go get him!"

In air-to-air kills, Captain Godfrey was only five behind Captain Gentile, an amazing record for a wingman.

Over Berlin, that day of the big raid, the 4th Air Group, and particularly Gentile and Godfrey, did itself proud.

As one box of B-17's made its run across the German capital, at least a hundred FW's and ME's jumped on it. The air above Berlin and for miles around was a gigantic arena where American and Nazi fighters tangled in scores of isolated actions. The hundred Germans that came out of the sun at the B-17's were a reserve unit, held back to clobber formations of bombers which reached the heart of the city. Between the Germans and the bombers were two lone Mustangs, piloted by Gentile and Godfrey.

Without hesitation they drove into the gaggle of ME's and FW's. Godfrey pulled out with two FW-190's below and to his right.

"You get 'em," Gentile said promptly. "I'll cover."

Godfrey's fast Mustang closed the gap and fired a burst at the wingman of the German element.

"Pour it on!" Gentile crowed.

The FW took bad hits on the flaps and rudder. It began to roll crazily in the air, then dove out of control.

Now Gentile gunned his Mustang ahead of Godfrey and chased the lead plane.

"Be my guest!" Godfrey called to him.

The FW turned right, but Gentile turned inside of it and caught it with a long burst from the two o'clock position.

"Bandits at eleven o'clock," Godfrey sang out. You're closer than me."

"Roger. Stay with me."

Gentile's Mustang split-S and latched onto the rear of the Germans.

"Make it quick, Gentle [Gentile's nickname]," Godfrey said. "The bombers are in bad trouble!"

The bombers were shooting off red flares, a signal for fighter assistance.

"Roger." Gentile snapped off a fast burst at 150 yards. It was a lucky shot and the FW flamed up.

"Nice shooting, buddy," Godfrey said. "Now let's go help our big friends."

Three squadrons of Nazi fighters were worrying the box of bombers as they maneuvered to release their eggs on the target. Flying wing to wing, the Mustangs hurtled into the swarm of FW's and ME's. Their combined firepower—sixteen guns—raked the tight formations. Two of the German planes took fire and peeled off right and left. Seconds later the pilots flipped them over and bailed out.

The Germans were furious now, and temporarily abandoned the bombers to concentrate on the brash twosome of Mustangs.

"Break, Johnny! Break right!" Gentile shouted.

Godfrey spun on one wing and two FW's shot past him, blasting empty air. Godfrey's turn enabled him to return the favor to Gentile.

"You break, Gentle! Trouble from four o'clock!"

Gentile shook the FW, and as it shot past him, Godfrey took up the chase right behind it. The German gunned his motor and dove. Godfrey stayed with him, pouring all of the Mustang's power on. But he couldn't get in close enough for a fatal shot. Gentile brought up the rear, covering his mate.

With the ground looming up fast, Godfrey tried to estimate just how far the FW would go before bringing its nose up again. It couldn't keep this up much longer. At a thousand feet Godfrey eased up on the throttle and his dive became more shallow. It was perfect judgment. The German pulled out at seven hundred feet and climbed in a steep trajectory that brought his ship spread-eagled in the Mustang's sight.

Godfrey held the trigger down and watched the tracers hit home. Then the guns burped out, and the FW was still alive.

"You finish him off, Gentle!" he told his leader.

Gentile was happy to oblige. The crippled FW could not run away from him, and seconds later he blew the tail assembly off the German plane.

"Well, we got us six bandits," Gentile declared. "I think that's par for the day. Let's pop back to merry old England and have a spot of tea."

Godfrey snorted. "Tea! Like hell!"

The bombers had unloaded their sticks, and were running for home. Other American fighter groups held the Germans off. So Gentile and Godfrey called it a day.

The first American daylight raid on Berlin could not be called an unqualified success. Seventy B-17's, twelve fighter planes and seven hundred men were lost that day. German losses had been extremely heavy, too, and the *Luftwaffe* had not been able to prevent the Americans from reaching the target.

Hermann Göring had been proved a liar in the eyes of the German people. More important, the Americans had proved to themselves—and the skeptical British— that it could be done. It was the beginning of round-the-clock bombing of the German capital which ultimately shattered German morale and upset Hitler's regime earlier than could be anticipated.

There would be greater air battles over Berlin—as many as two-thousand bombers and one-thousand escort fighters engaged—but the raid on March 6, 1944, "Big-B," was the most significant. The die of defeat had been cast for the *Luftwaffe* and the Third Reich. And Blakeslee's Debden Gangsters and Zemke's Wolfpack added scores of miniature swastikas to the impressive blocks of "notches" already decorating the fuselages of their Mustangs and Thunderbolts.

16.

THE GREAT ALLIED AIR BLITZ against Germany in 1944-45 was not strictly an Eighth Air Force show. As part of the build-up in England for the invasion of Europe, the Ninth Tactical Air Force was brought in from the Mediterranean Theater to support the Eighth.

The Ninth, which had covered the landings in Sicily and Italy, was geared primarily to provide air support for ground troops. As such, it did not get in on the spectacular Berlin raids, nor did its aces have the opportunity to rack up scores like Gabreski, Johnson and Meyer. But whenever the pilots of the Ninth got a chance to tangle with enemy fighters, they made the most of it.

Shortly after the breakthrough of Patton's Third Army at Avranches, the 354th Fighter Group of the Ninth was running interference for the tankers, bombing and strafing enemy columns. The Americans were flying P-51's and F-38 fighter-bombers (converted P-38 Lightnings) with two five-hundred-pound bombs slung beneath the wings.

Before it could attack its target, the 354th was jumped by 105 Messerschmitts. Now with the odds only two to one against his boys, group leader Colonel Eagleston wasn't too worried. The Mustangs and F-38's were more than a match for the ME-109's. Naturally, they had to jettison the bombs before attempting to mix it up in a dogfight.

"Kick belly tanks and payload," Eagleston gave the

word. Then to his wingman, Lieutenant Fred Couch: "Cover me, Fred. I'm going in!"

Couch's squawking reply was lost on Eagleston in the scream of his power dive and the chatter of German guns. As his Mustang hooked onto the tail of an ME, another ME skidded in behind the group leader. With satisfaction, he heard the comforting sound of his wingman's guns. He glanced back and saw the German slide away steaming burning fuel.

"Good boy!" he radioed Couch.

"Listen, Colonel—" Couch began, but again the voice was eclipsed by the noise and excitement of combat.

Eagleston flamed his German as the ME tried to climb into an Immelmann. Then he flew into the center of a flight of four ME's, who immediately formed a Lufbery circle around him. Eagleston split-S to twenty thousand feet, pulled up sharply and twisted his Mustang into a half-loop, then Immelmanned out in the opposite direction. A brilliant display of aerobatics that baffled the pursuing Germans.

Wingman Couch hung on like Scotch tape through it all. Lucky, too, for an ME came sneaking out of the sun and blasted away at Eagleston from a hundred yards. Couch came to the rescue again, riddling the German with holes and chasing him back into the cloud cover.

Eagleston reflected that the wingman was the unsung hero of the air arena. Not too long though, for he was in a gaggle of Germans again, maneuvering for position. A deflection shot caught an ME amidships and it rolled over and died. Couch scared off two others who were attempting to cut in on the colonel. A group of ten dove on them now, and Eagleston called to Couch: "Let's show these Jerries what the Mustang can do."

He proceeded to put the P-51 through a string of stunts that would have won the admiration of a test pilot. The Germans gave up, but wingman Couch stayed with him all the way. The colonel could not help but admire the tenacity and quick reflexes of the young lieutenant. It is no simple matter to play follow-the-leader at 450 miles per hour.

Eagleston scored his third kill of the day and Couch added another to his tally. Throughout the battle he had never left his colonel unguarded. Finally the Germans, who had suffered the loss of twenty-four Messerschmitts in the fierce battle, fled back across the Rhine.

Mightily pleased with the performance of his boys—and especially pleased with himself—Eagleston gave his wingman a pat on the back verbally.

"Pretty good flying, Fred," he said with reserve. "I really wrung hell out of this baby, but you did a fine job of staying with me."

"Colonel," Couch said in exasperation, "I've been trying to tell you all along—I couldn't shake loose my bombs. Lucky thing for me you didn't get too fancy, or I never would have been able to stay with you."

Astonished, Colonel Eagleston looked toward the P-51 of his wingman, coming up alongside now. Sure enough, there were the two five-hundred-pounders sitting snugly under the wings.

"Yeah," he said in a hollow voice. "Lucky thing I didn't get too fancy."

Later, Eagleston admitted: "That really took the wind out of my sails!"

Colonel Eagleston went on to become the leading ace of the Ninth Air Force with twenty-three German planes destroyed.

Another hero of the Ninth was Major James H. Howard. Howard was an old sidekick of Pappy Boyington's from the days of the Flying Tigers. He is the only ace to score in both the European and Pacific Theaters, shooting down six Japs over China and six Germans over Europe.

Leading a group of Mustangs on an escort mission over Oschersleben, Germany, Howard gave a performance that won him the Congressional Medal of Honor.

Just before they reached the target, Howard's group was jumped by a superior force of ME-110's, and soon the Mustangs were scattered all over the sky in isolated scraps. In the meantime, a second batch of thirty FW's sprang on the unprotected bombers and prevented them from dropping their eggs.

Howard blasted the wing off one ME, sent another running, then returned to see how the big friends were making out. It wasn't good. He started to put out a "Mayday" call to regroup his fighters, then figured it would be too late to do the bombers any good.

Grimly, he turned his P-51 and waded into the thirty German fighters singlehanded. The ferocity and brashness of his attack rattled the Germans. They could not believe one lone Mustang would have been so foolish, and kept looking up into the sun for the rest of the Americans.

While they were looking, Howard cut in behind an element of FW's and went to work. His first burst sent one down. The other dove, and Howard let it go. There were abundant targets all around him. Actually the Germans were handicapped by their own numbers. An FW raced at the Mustang; Howard flipped away and the German's burst cut into one of his own comrades. Howard kicked rudder left and right as a formation of FW's loomed ahead of him. The spraying slugs killed one and crippled two other planes. They limped out of the battle.

In the confusion, the bombers got away from the Germans and unloaded their payload over Oschersleben.

Howard's P-51 had gaping holes in the fuselage and wings, but miraculously, it had not taken a vital hit. Three of the guns conked out, but the others did double duty. Before it was over, another FW spun in a smoky spiral to earth, and still others were forced out of the fight by the damage the fighting major had inflicted on them. At last, other Mustangs came to his rescue and routed the remainder of the FW's.

Howard limped home where he was acclaimed "Jim the Giant Killer." Piloting his P-51, Major Howard had dealt the *Luftwaffe* one of the worst defeats it had ever suffered in aerial combat.

The Ninth Air Force did not produce the impressive array of aces that the Eighth Air Force did, but it produced some unusual ones.

Captain Richard Turner was leading a squadron of P-51 fighters across the English Channel one day when his wingman reported: "Bogey twelve o'clock high! Man, is he coming in fast!"

Turner squinted through the windshield. The approaching aircraft had a needle nose. "Looks like an ME," he said slowly.

"Chrissakes!" another pilot said. "It ain't got any wings!"

Every pair of eyeballs in the squadron bulged as the unidentified craft closed the gap with amazing speed. A leaden lump settled in Turner's belly as he recognized the distinctive fins at the tail of the long wingless cylinder. There was no mistake now.

"That's no plane," Turner said tensely. "That's a buzz bomb!"

Shortly after D-Day Hitler had unleashed his long-awaited "secret weapon" against England, the famed V-2 rocket. The V-2 was strictly a terror device, with little strategic value because, unlike the modern-day guided missile, there was no way to aim the rocket. The Germans just dumped them vindictively all over the English countryside.

Reaching an apogee of one hundred miles, in rare cases, the "buzz bomb"—named because of the peculiar whine of its jet engine—would descend on target in a long glide. That blood-chilling sound gave England nightmares; rather the sudden cut-off of the sound, for when the engine stopped that meant the V-2 was about to nose down. During June, 1944, and for three months after, buzz bombs rained down on London and other English cities indiscriminately, killing thousands of people.

There was virtually no defense against the V-2, because of the high altitude and high speed at which it traveled. No aircraft could match this performance, except for a brief period as it descended blindly on the target.

Captain Turner and his squadron were experiencing the rare privilege of witnessing one of the monsters in the dying moments of its flight.

Turner cursed aloud. It was midday. The streets of London would be jammed. Shoppers, autos, children on their way home from school. Dozens, maybe hundreds, had no way of knowing that their names were on this incoming bomb.

"All right, you guys!" Turner said. "Let's give it the old college try! Maybe we'll have one pass at this thing. That's all! Nobody gets a second chance."

The projectile was nosing down below the formation now, and the Mustangs peeled off and split-S at high speed to intercept it.

Turner saw he was not leading it enough, and kicked hard on the rudder. The P-51 skidded to the left in a steep dive. At four hundred yards, he fingered the trigger and held it, watching the tracers arc way out in front of the bomb. He held his breath as the V-2 streaked into the 50's. Perfect deflection shots! Abruptly the bomb disappeared in a ball of fire! He felt the Mustang buck under the shock wave. Shrapnel beat a tattoo on the fuselage.

"Nice work, boss," a voice cut in on the radio.

Turner's heart was suddenly light. He would finish the war with twelve kills, but none of the others would ever give him the pride and satisfaction this one had. That night a host of faceless men, women and children sat down at their supper tables by the grace of Captain Richard Turner—and God.

In the days after that—until advancing Allied Armies captured the V-2 launch sites—the deadly buzz bombs became one of the most coveted of "kills" among the pilots of the RAF and the USAF.

Captain James Daglish led American aces at this nerve-racking game, with three buzz bombs shot down.

17.

PROBABLY THE MOST unusual ace to achieve fame in the European Theater was Staff Sergeant Benjamin Warner, the only man of his rank to rate such an honor.

Staff Sergeant Warner was gunner in a B-17 Fortress of the Twelfth Air Force operating in northern Italy. On one mission Warner's bomber group and fighter escort were jumped by overwhelming numbers of FW-190's and ME-109's. The American fighters had their hands full protecting themselves, and the B-17's were soon isolated and at the mercy of a swarm of Germans.

The Forts put up a good show with their ten guns apiece, but they were still no match for the speedy fighters ripping in and out like killer sharks.

"Bandit coming in at five o'clock!" another gunner radioed to Warner.

There is no lonelier spot in the world than the gun turret of a B-17, hanging out in space like a goldfish in a bowl. Warner swiveled to meet the threat, and held his breath as the FW rushed in toward him, spitting fire from the lead edges of its wings. He braced himself for the shatter of plexiglass and the rending of lead at his flesh, letting the German plane fill up his sight.

Hard on the trigger! Tracers arched out from the 50-caliber, felt for the FW and found it. The German skidded out of sight, trailing flame and smoke.

A second FW was right behind it. Warner didn't even let up on the trigger. This 190 ran into the barrage of 50's before he could get off a burst. Warner recoiled in his cramped compartment as the German maintained a collision course, but at the last instant the FW flipped over and skidded away, burning from a leaky fuel tank.

The 190's were coming in from all sides now. The B-17's crewmen yelled back and forth to each other.

"Watch that baby at six high!"

"Two bandits at nine low!"

"Jesus! I got another!" Warner crowed.

"Good work, you sonov—" The words were clipped off as an FW found the mark, killing one of Warner's fellow gunners.

There was a small fire up forward. The B-17 reeled under the pasting it was getting from the Nazi fighters, but it was the hardiest ship any Air Force ever put aloft.

Tracers floated toward Warner, but fell low before they reached the target. The FW pilot lifted his nose, but before his slugs found the mark, Warner caught him in the engine, and the FW exploded.

Although the temperature in his fishbowl was below zero, Warner was sweating from every pore in his body.

Time and time again, the fearsome tracers came so

close it seemed as though he could reach out and catch the big fiery balls. But there was no time for fear.

Back and forth the tail guns swiveled, pumping like the pistons in a V-8.

"Watch it Ben! Two bandits nine high!"

The other guns on the left side of the ship had been silenced. Warner couldn't get his gun far enough around to get the enemy planes in the sights, and watched helplessly as they raked the Fort amidships.

Then they peeled off to the right and into his guns. Warner worked the 50's into the flashing targets with malicious glee. Bull's-eye on the cockpit! The pilotless ship rolled over and fell away. A second burst of deflection shots stitched a design the length of the second FW. It disintegrated from a direct hit in a fuel tank.

It was over as suddenly as it had began. The American fighters had won their fight and raced back to rescue the big friends. The Germans gave it up and turned north for home. As the last FW peeled off from the fight, he swung too wide and for a beautiful moment was framed in Warner's sight—a big cross against the blue. Warner squeezed the trigger and watched the tracers hit home. The FW spun like a top and fell off with a ribbon of smoke twisting in its wake. Number seven for Warner—*in one day!*

For his unusual achievement, Sergeant Warner was honored by the theater commander by having his name included in the official list of Twelfth Air Force Aces. The sharpshooting gunner lived up to his fame by downing another two German fighters before he closed out his career.

PART FIVE

The Last Gasp of the Luftwaffe

18.

THE V-2 ROCKET was one of two cards Hitler had up his sleeve in the last year of the war. Fortunately for the Allies, he elected to play the V-2 as his hole card, and ignored the "ace," which might have won the game for Germany, until it was too late.

Late in the fall of 1944, a patrol of the Ninth Tactical Air Force was flying over the Nazi lines when the squadron leader alerted his team:

"Two bogeys, seven o'clock high."

His eyes remained riveted on the oncoming planes as they approached at phenomenal speed. At first he thought they were buzz bombs, although it was unheard of for V-2's to travel in pairs. Then, as they came into range he saw that they were winged aircraft, with the needle noses of the Messerschmitt. But no ME he had ever encountered could make this kind of time. There was something else very strange about the craft, too, as expressed by the excited squawking from the other pilots.

"Skipper! Am I nuts or something? Them bandits don't have any props!"

The captain's stomach did a flip-flop. It was true. The planes did not show evidence of having any propellers. They were Messerschmitts all right—black crosses on the wings, the swastika on the tail—with what appeared to be twin engines slung beneath the wings. But the engines had no props; just empty, black air scoops. Then it came to him! This must be the new German fighter he had heard rumors about, a fighter reputed to be powered by jet engines—the same principal as the V-2 rockets, he imagined, but under human guidance.

"Strip for action!" he ordered his pilots. Sixteen Mustangs jettisoned belly tanks. Gun switches and sights were primed.

The oncoming jets flashed past the squadron on the left and banked to cut in behind the Mustangs—the classic maneuver of fighters. There were four flights of P-51's, and the tail-end flight responded with the classic answer to the ME's' maneuver: it turned tight left into the Germans' turn.

"Greased lightning" is a trite phrase, but it is the only way to describe the ensuing action. When the Nazi pilots advanced throttle, the Americans realized with awe that they had been merely cruising before. In a blur the two jets whizzed past them, turned at virtually right angles and pulled up right behind the other three flights of the American squadron.

"Break!" the colonel screamed to his men, and the Mustangs split to right and left in the tight, high-speed turns that had always shaken off the conventional ME's and FW's in the past.

But there was no shaking off these babies. The jets played with the P-51's the way an ME-109 could play with an awkward bomber. Their wing guns crackled and two Mustangs caught fire.

The American squadron leader experienced the sick panic of helplessness. A few minutes of dueling with the strangely shrieking planes with no propellers convinced him that even at odds of seven to one the Mustangs— the best fighter in the USAF—were no match for the Germans. He ordered his pilots to form a Lufbery circle, each ship holding close to the tail of the ship in front in an enormous daisy chain so that none of them were exposed at the rear.

Even the Lufbery failed to discourage the jets. Diving through the circle and climbing up to dive again, they made pass after pass at the Mustangs, blasting with cannons and machine guns. Deflection shots flamed two more P-51's and crippled three more. Desperately, the Mustangs counterattacked but their deflection shots always fell far behind the racing Germans, and, of course, there was no hope of catching them from the rear.

At last the Nazi planes ran out of ammo and abandoned the game with a jaunty salute of their wings. Badly shaken, the colonel led his decimated squadron back to base. Only twelve of the original sixteen remained and three of these were seriously damaged.

The lights burned until dawn at Supreme Headquarters that night. Our Air Force brass was plenty worried. It was a worry that was contagious—all the way up to General Eisenhower.

"We won't have anything to compete with the ME-262 for another year," one general voiced the opinion.

"That isn't good enough," said Colonel J. P. Henry, a group commander in the Eighth Air Force. "We've got to lick this problem now—tomorrow, the day after that."

"My God!" said a jittery general. "If the Jerries can produce the ME-262 in mass, the *Luftwaffe* will put us out of business."

"How can we fight them?" a staff officer asked hopelessly.

"Not in the air, that's for sure," said Henry. "You know what Joe Louis said about Billy Conn: 'He can run, but he can't hide.' Same with these jets. They have to light sometime. That's our only answer. We've got to catch them on the ground. Raise hell with the German airfields where they're housed."

"And continue to pound the German factories where they're made, the way we used to look for rattlesnake dens down in Texas," another general said grimly. "Destroy 'em before they're full-grown."

This, then, became the priority mission of the USAF in the last six months of the war: Get the ME-262! As an incentive to the pilots, it was decreed that an airplane destroyed on the ground would rate as an equal kill to one destroyed in the air.

The brass was not being magnanimous. The fact was that strafing and dive-bombing enemy airfields was actually more dangerous than the average dogfight. It was bad enough to fly through a barrage of antiaircraft fire at twenty thousand feet. At twenty feet it was near suicidal! Not only were the gun batteries firing at point-blank range, but the attacking planes were vulnerable to small-arms fire of rifles and machine guns. There were other hazards: trees, high-tension wires and uneven terrain; many a Mustang and Thunderbolt limped home with its prop tips bent and blunted from trying to dig a hole in some knoll or building cornice.

This was a concept of warfare which the Germans themselves had introduced in World War I. The "strafing" attack is derived from the German word *strafen*— "to punish." And in the last months and weeks of World War II, the USAF punished the German airfields and factories where the amazing ME-262 jet fighters were hangared and produced. American losses were high, but the new "baby" of the *Luftwaffe* had to be destroyed before it grew up into a "monster."

In this struggle, no fighter group in the Eighth played a more vital role than the 339th, commanded by J. P. Henry.

On April 15th, the 339th escorted a group of B-17's into Germany to bomb Munich. It was suspected that an underground factory somewhere outside the city limits was turning out the Messerschmitt jet fighter, but neither aerial reconnaissance photographs nor intelligence reports could pinpoint the location of the plant. The mission was to clobber anything that looked suspicious.

After the raid was over Major Joseph Thury and two flights of Mustangs tipped their wings to the returning bombers and set out on a brief patrol of the surrounding countryside. There was nothing to shoot at that day in the way of airborne enemy fighters, so Thury led his band in a wide sweep to the south of Munich and headed home.

Then the major saw something that piqued his curiosity. At first glance it appeared to be an ordinary forest clearing, but closer study convinced him that its contours were too regular and linear for a natural development.

"Let's make a pass at it and see what's up," he ordered his eight Mustangs.

"Kind of low on gas, Joe," his wingman reminded him.

"This won't take long, I think," Thury said. "We can't afford to pass up anything at this stage."

He tipped his P-51 into a split-S, pulling out above the edge of the clearing at about five hundred feet. His eyes narrowed and his heart accelerated. German fighter planes were huddled under the canopy of foliage that ran along both long sides of the field. Blunt-nosed FW-190's, ME-110's and—the unmistakable silhouette of the Messerschmitt jets! He didn't know how many of them, but they outnumbered the other aircraft.

The Mustang raced over the strip, all six 50's belching fire. The heavy slugs kicked up so much dust he couldn't tell what, if anything, he had hit. He cleared the trees at the end of the clearing and climbed in a wide turn to the left.

He watched the other seven planes make their passes, their tracers glittering among the leafy boughs which hung above the German fighters like bulbs on a Christmas tree. Nazi antiaircaft batteries at the four corners of the field threw up sporadic fire at the passing Mustangs, scant protection for a rich prize like this, Thury thought.

There was gas and ammo for one more pass, then Major Thury gave the word to break off the attack.

"We'll be back," he told his boys. "The sooner, the better."

That night he conferred with the 339th CO, Colonel Henry. Both agreed that it had been the chance of a lifetime.

"If only we hadn't shot half our wad of gas and ammo on the escort mission," Thury lamented, "we might have won the whole pot. There must have been two hundred fighters on that field. Maybe seventy-five to one-hundred jets."

Henry shook his head. "They must be fresh from that damned factory. I hate to think what will happen when they are operational—one hundred, good Lord!"

"We can still finish the job," Thury said. "Tomorrow."

Henry looked at him knowingly. "I don't imagine I have to tell you what kind of reception will be waiting for you tomorrow. The Germans know the cat is out of the bag. They won't have time to move those new planes, but they'll have gun batteries lined up hub to hub around the field."

"I don't see where we have any choice, sir. We've got to give it a try."

"I know." Henry sighed. "Good luck."

Before sunup the sixteen Mustangs of Major Thury's 505th Squadron were warming up. At 0700 hours the squadron was airborne. Two hours later it was approaching Munich at twenty thousand feet.

One by one the four flights peeled off to the south, silver wings flashing in the sunlight. Ahead, Thury spotted the field.

"Upper Leader calling. Ditch those wing tanks!"

Simultaneously in sixteen Mustangs, hands reached for gun and sight switches. Thury nosed the P-51 down.

"I'll lead the first flight in. The rest of you stay on top until we find out what the score is."

The Mustang hurtled down on the field, which looked as innocent as it had the day before. The major's eyes flicked around the perimeter, expecting all hell to break out as the seconds ticked off. Maybe the Germans had goofed? Maybe they hadn't bothered to beef up the ack-ack batteries? It didn't make sense, but when his finger tightened on the trigger, not a single golf ball of orange fire had appeared.

Thury raced across the edge of the field, spewing 50's through the camouflage covering the German fighters. The three Mustangs behind him made their passes, and all four climbed away unscathed.

"Hot dawg!" his wingman cried gleefully. "Them old Jerries have just given up and pulled out it looks like."

"I wonder," Thury said hesitantly.

Still there was nothing to indicate otherwise. "Okay," he said into the mike. "This is Upper Leader. Next time we all go down."

The Mustangs peeled off in flights of four, sixteen Mustangs slicing down in power dives. Again Thury was first on target, lining up the tightly packed German fighters in his sights. His Mustang had just cleared the edge of the field when the "hell" he had been expecting erupted from all sides. This was literally a wall of fire and steel. Bursting shells, heavy machine guns, rifles, flaming 20-mm. balls that exploded and filled the air with flying shrapnel.

Thury breezed through it miraculously without taking a hit, his guns working incessantly. An FW exploded, followed by an ME-262 jet, then another jet caught fire. At the edge of the field he climbed away at high speed.

Circling he watched breathlessly as the other P-51's

ran the gantlet. One, two, three, four, five—he began to breath again—then a Mustang burst into flame and nosed down, exploding on the ground.

Christ!

Never had he seen the Germans defend an airfield so viciously and desperately. They wanted to save those jets real bad.

Thury couldn't conceive how they had positioned so many guns in such a limited area. Then he saw tracers arcing, it seemed, right out of the treetops. Gun platforms in the trees! They had thought of everything! Another Mustang flamed out and crashed beyond the field in the trees.

"This is Upper Leader! Attention!" he briefed the men as they reorganized out of range of the ack-ack guns for another pass. "Forget the planes for the time being. First we're gonna knock out those guns!"

A second time Thury's Mustang led the way in. On this pass, the Mustangs sprayed the tree platforms and the gun emplacements at the corners of the field. A third pass. A fourth. A fifth. The ground fire was diminishing now. Hundreds of German gunners were chewed up by the big 50's.

"Okay. Now let's get back to work," Thury announced, when he was satisfied that ground fire presented a minimum hazard.

The Mustangs shot across the field, silver streaks with fire jetting out of their noses. Thury counted a dozen ME-216's burning; countless others.

A fifth pass, a sixth. On the seventh he could no longer keep count of the destruction on the ground. German gunners, who had fled the deadly attack of the Mustangs, crept back to their posts. On the eighth pass, Thury ran into heavy ack-ack fire. A shell ripped off his right wing tip. Slugs and shrapnel slashed through the fuselage and canopy, chewing up the instrument panel and narrowly missing Thury. The wounded ship lurched to the right, dropping fast. Desperately he kicked the rudder hard left and fought the stick. He just got her nose up before he reached the trees. Branches scraped the P-51's belly as she struggled for altitude.

"I'm hit bad," Thury radioed his second in command, Major Tower. "You take over."

"Can you make it?" came back anxiously.

Thury grinned. "On the well-known 'wing and a prayer' if I'm lucky . . . So long, and—give 'em hell!"

The 505th did give 'em hell, and before that day was over they left sixty enemy fighters ablaze on the field. It was one of the most devastating blows dealt out to the *Luftwaffe*, struggling to regain control of the air with its amazing ME jet fighter.

The Germans might have done it, too, if it had not been for the daring of men like Lieutenant Colonel Joseph Thury and the others in his squadron, who helped stifle the jet project in its infancy. At the war's end, Colonel Thury and his 505th Squadron had destroyed more enemy planes than any other squadron of the Eighth Air Force.

CONCLUSION

IN A SENSE, World War II wrote *finis* to the Golden Age of the "dogfight" in the way the younger generation and their fathers and grandfathers like to think about it. The age of the atom and supersonic jet has removed the vital element of glamour from aerial war—if it can be said that there ever was any glamour in war. The "human factor" might be a better way to express it.

Undeniably war has been "hell" from the day two cavemen paired off to do combat with a pair of hostile cavemen. But through all the horror ran a golden thread of romance, personal courage, *esprit de corps*, the close comradeship of men fighting for a cause they believed was worthy. A man of skill and courage, a strong man could endure and triumph over the peril of combat. This was particularly true for the aviator in World Wars I and II.

In a fighter plane, the dimensions of war were reduced to the basics—man versus man, the way it had been before the advent of gunpowder. This was war at its most personal level. The foot soldier seldom saw the enemy he killed—or who killed him—close up. In a dogfight it was different. The enemy was an intimate. You met him on equal terms, and if he was more skillful than you, the victory would go to him. It seemed a nobler way to die than bleeding to death in a shell hole from a chance bullet or mortar burst.

Modern weapons have changed all that irrevocably. Even in the Korean War, fighter planes dueled at high speeds that prohibited dependence on human reflexes to fire machine guns and cannon. Radar sights and electronically operated triggers made the pilot an incidental factor in the cockpit of a fighter plane. True, his flying skill counted for something, as evidenced by the great aces who emerged from the Korean conflict, but somehow the glamour was tarnished. He was a highly skilled technician first, a "killer" second.

More recent developments in aircraft have all but eclipsed that extra something the aces of the last two great wars seemed to possess. Fighters of the future will travel three and four times the speed of sound. Electronic devices will do most of the work for feeble man. The sidewinder missile, already in use, enables a fighter plane to fire his rockets blindly in pitch darkness, certain he will score a hit on any enemy in the vicinity. The sidewinder's infrared eye sniffs out the heat of the enemy's exhaust and climbs right up that exhaust stream for a bull's-eye. Awesome—but hardly romantic.

The aces of the past wars will be contemplated in future history alongside the heroes of Homer's *Iliad*. Their kind will not pass this way again. But their deeds are immortal.

The End

BIBLIOGRAPHY

Samurai by Saburo Sakai with Martin Caidan, E. P. Dutton, Inc.

Baa Baa Black Sheep by Gregory Boyington, G. P. Putnam's Sons

Wings of Victory by Ivor Halstead, E. P. Dutton, Inc.

American Aces by E. H. Sims, Harper & Brothers

Five Down and Glory by G. Gurney and M. Friedlander, Jr., G. P. Putnam's Sons

Army Air Forces of the World by W. F. Cronin

I Was a Nazi Flyer by G. Leski

Squadrons Up! by N. Monks

U.S.A.F. Historical Division, Research Studies Institute, Maxwell Field

Air Force Museum, Wright Patterson Air Force Base

Japanese Air Defense Force

Federal Republic of Germany Air Force

Department of the Air Force, Book and Magazine Section

Department of the Navy, Book and Magazine Section

Department of the Army, Book and Magazine Section

Daily Fighter Victory Credit Board Results

United States Air Force Academy Library

Flying Magazine

Saga Magazine

Climax Magazine

Time Magazine
Newsweek Magazine
Life Magazine
The New York *Times*
The New York *Daily News*
U.S.A.F. Public Information Office, New York City
The Encyclopaedia Britannica

It Was Called Operation Shingle—

A Desperate Gamble That Turned

Into A Fight For Survival

The Battle Of Anzio

By T. R. Fehrenbach

Foreword by William H. Simpson
General, U. S. Army, Retired

No troops ever fought with more gallantry, against greater odds than the Allied forces on the beach at Anzio. Casualties mounted hourly, reaching staggering totals, and still they held the blood-soaked beachhead. It was grinding infantry warfare at its worst.

Pinned down on a narrow strip of sand, harassed by German planes, artillery shells, small-arms and mortar fire, and charging unmanned tanks loaded with high explosives, these tired men were pushed to the limit of human endurance.

Here is a dramatic true account of that battle, from ill-starred beginning to triumphant ending, told with understanding, deep pride and deeper humility, and showing the indomitable fighting spirit of the Allied dogface soldier.

A MONARCH AMERICANA BOOK

Available at all newsstands and bookstores   50¢

If you are unable to secure this book at your local dealer, you may obtain a copy by sending 50¢ plus 5¢ for handling to Monarch Books, Inc., Mail Order Department, Capital Building, Derby, Connecticut.

Now—You Can Read These Famous
MONARCH AMERICANA
BOOKS

MA304 **THE WICKED, WICKED WOMEN**   by James Kendricks 35¢ ☐
Loves and hatreds of the women who followed the Erie Canal, in
the days of Buffalo's Canal Street and the "Big Ditch."

MA305 **BLOOD-AND-GUTS PATTON**   by Jack Pearl 35¢ ☐
The swashbuckling life story of America's most daring and con-
troversial general.

MA306 **BREAKTHROUGH**   by Franklin M. Davis, Jr. 35¢ ☐
The epic story of the Battle of the Bulge, the greatest pitched
battle in America's history.

MA307 **THE LINDBERGH KIDNAPPING CASE**   by Ovid Demaris 35¢ ☐
The true story of the crime that shocked the world and touched
off history's greatest manhunt.

MA308 **THE SAM HOUSTON STORY**   by Dean Owen 35¢ ☐
The swashbuckling account of the man whose daring exploits
altered the course of Texan history.

MA309 **THE APACHE WARS**   by John Conway 35¢ ☐
Exciting true saga of the bloody conflict between the white men
and the Apache Indians on the Southwest frontier.

MA310 **HAREM ISLAND**   by Anthony Sterling 35¢ ☐
Astounding true story of a self-proclaimed saint who made religion
a business and turned sin into a virtue.

MA311 **THE DILLINGER STORY**   by Ovid Demaris 35¢ ☐
Here is the dramatic story of Dillinger—gangster, bank robber,
killer and Public Enemy No. 1!

MA312 **THE KENNEDY CABINET**   by Deane and David Heller 35¢ ☐
With foreword by The Honorable A. S. Mike Monroney, U. S.
Senator from Oklahoma. Dramatic profiles of our Cabinet depart-
ment heads and their jobs.

MA313 **"BABY FACE" NELSON**   by Steve Thurman 35¢ ☐
Thrilling account of the crime career of one of America's most
notorious modern-day badmen.

MA314 **AMERICA'S WAR HEROES**   by Jay Scott 35¢ ☐
Dramatic tales of courageous service men whose exploits won them
The Congressional Medal of Honor.

MONARCH BOOKS, INC.   MA1
Mail Order Department
Division Street
Derby, Connecticut

Please send me the books checked. I enclose cash ☐, check ☐,

money order ☐ (check appropriate box) in the amount of

............, plus .... coupons to cover the purchase

of .... books.

Name ....

Address ....

City .... Zone ...... State ....

☐ Check here if you would like to receive a copy of our
    latest complete catalogue.

A Memorable Novel of the
Lafayette Flying Corps of
World War I Fame

Falcons Of France

By Charles Nordoff and James Norman Hall

Authors of MUTINY ON THE BOUNTY

and

MEN AGAINST THE SEA

It was the dark and bloody spring of 1918. The Germans were on the move again, pushing forward in a devastating drive to break the back of Allied resistance. Overhead flew the German Fokkers, providing cover for their on-rushing infantry.

Into the battle roared the daring men of the famed Lafayette Flying Corps piloting Spads held together with "spit and string." Outnumbered and fighting against superior firepower, they turned the tide of battle to write a glorious page in the history of World War I.

"It is more than a good yarn—it is a living and consequently better history of the Lafayette Squadron"—
ATLANTIC BOOKSHELF

A Special Fiction Headliner from

MONARCH BOOKS, INC.

Available at all newsstands and bookstores 35¢

If you are unable to secure this book at your local dealer, you may obtain a copy by sending 35¢ plus 5¢ for handling to Monarch Books, Inc., Mail Order Department, Capital Building, Division Street, Derby, Conn.

A Savagely Realistic Novel of Treachery and

Torture in a Jap Prisoner-of-War Camp

BAMBOO CAMP #10

By Franklin M. Davis, Jr.

Author of BREAKTHROUGH

Bamboo Camp #10 was reserved for Americans captured in the Burmese Campaign. It was run by the dregs of the Japanese Army and serviced by slave girls imported from Bangkok.

This is the story of one of its prisoners—Lieutenant Harley Frazier—the torments he endured at the hands of his lust-crazed captors, his life-and-death struggle with his sadistic CO, and the betrayal of his escape plans by his own fellow countrymen!

Until a native girl, brought in to pleasure the camp guards, turned to Frazier for help, and unexpectedly provided the means for a daring breakout.

A New Bestselling War Novel From

MONARCH BOOKS, INC.

Available at all newsstands and bookstores   35¢

If you are unable to secure this book at your local dealer, you may obtain a copy by sending 35¢ plus 5¢ for handling to Monarch Books, Inc., Mail Order Department, Capital Building, Derby, Connecticut.

Complete Reading Enjoyment

IN THESE

MONARCH Human Behavior Books